The
CIVIL WAR
In the Words of Its Greatest Commanders

The CIVIL WAR

In the Words of Its Greatest Commanders

Personal Memoirs of U.S. Grant

Memoirs of Robert E. Lee

by Armistead L. Long

JG PRESS

PAGE 2: Ulysses S. Grant.

OPPOSITE: Robert E. Lee and Thomas "Stonewall" Jackson.

PAGES 4–5: Battle of the Wilderness.

PAGES 10–11: The Fall of Petersburg.

Published by World Publications Group, Inc.
140 Laurel Street
East Bridgewater, MA 02333
www.wrldpub.com

Reprinted 2011 by World Publications Group, Inc.
Copyright © 2002

ISBN-13: 978-1-57215-818-4
ISBN-10: 1-57215-818-2

Printed and bound in China by Toppan Leefung Printing Limited.

Chihuahua. A third force, under Colonel Stephen Watts Kearny, would head west, take Santa Fe, and end up in San Diego on the California coast.

These columns were all victorious. As they moved, Taylor's men were repeatedly engaged, but drove Mexican forces before them. Grant, meanwhile, had been made quartermaster of his regiment, but constantly sought to be near the front. During the siege of Monterrey, his brigade was pinned down, and he volunteered to carry this news to higher headquarters. He took the written message and galloped through hostile fire, hanging from the saddle on one side of his horse like the trick rider he was.

Wool's force eventually joined that of Taylor, and on February 23, 1847, Taylor defeated a much larger force at Buena Vista. All that remained was the capture of the national capital, Mexico City. General Winfield Scott led the force that would achieve this purpose, and after it landed at Vera Cruz it fought its way inland.

Lee's actions in the Mexican War had a somewhat higher profile than those of Grant. Although he was only a captain and, as such, a very junior officer, Lee had graduated from West Point fourteen years before Grant, and with his extensive experience in the army,

he was almost an officer from a different generation. Indeed, in Mexico, his performance of engineering duties was so exemplary that he soon was called to join Scott's staff. In that role, staff officers above him were awed by his intelligence and his abilities, and he was able to directly advise and guide the hand of General Scott.

BELOW: Taylor's forces take Monterrey in a crucial engagement of the Mexican War.

Once the U.S. forces had made their way to the edge of Mexico City, the first major challenge Scott faced was to find a way to take or bypass the seemingly impregnable Mexican defenses at San Augustin and San Antonio, two major fortresses on the road to Mexico City. Lee several times conducted personal, high-risk reconnaissance, both by day and by night, deep into territory held by Mexican forces. He several times hid as Mexican soldiers passed close by, thus risking discovery and death or captivity. And while jeopardizing the crucial eyes, ears, and brain of General Scott's most important adviser might have been criticized had he been killed or taken,

he was not, and he returned with plans to flank Mexican forces with surprise attacks.

Orders for the attacks followed, and Lee was with the troops as they confronted the obstacles he had warned of, such as ravines, canals, and the nearly impassable broken ground of the Pedregal. Lee showed them how to continue their advance, and during the night, while American soldiers rested, he twice crossed the two-mile-wide stretch of the Pedregal on foot. He did this to keep General Scott informed of the progress of his forces, and Lee was back with the infantry when they finally launched their attacks on Mexican positions the following morning.

RIGHT: Grant routs Mexican forces at San Cosme by mounting a howitzer in a church belfry.

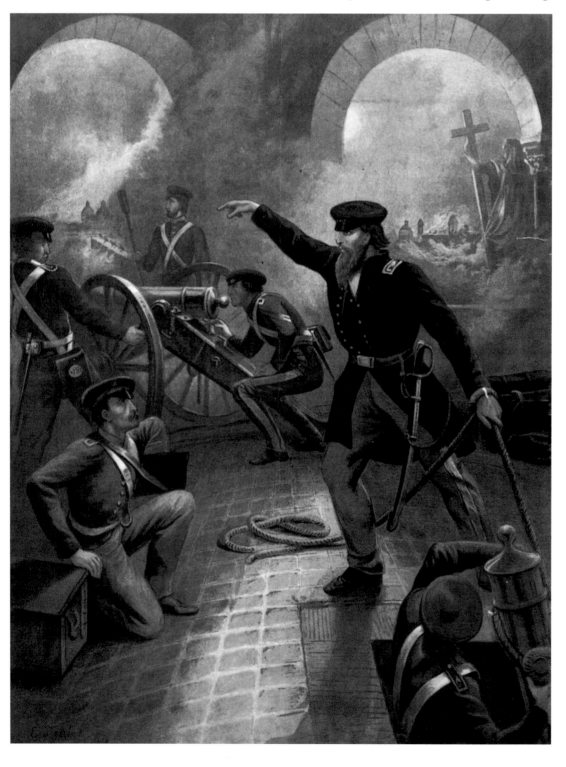

The attacks, of course, were successful.

This operation went on for several days, from around the 11th to the 20th of August, 1847, and Lee was heavily involved in every part of it, from reconnaissance to planning to execution. Every general in the American force had the highest praise for Lee, and when General Scott forwarded to Washington the names of those who deserved commendation, he named "Captain R.E. Lee (as distinguished for felicitous execution as for science and daring)." In later testimony before a court of inquiry, Scott would say that Captain Lee had there rendered "the greatest feat of physical and moral courage performed by any individual, in my knowledge, pending the campaign."

Lee was to receive three brevet promotions for his actions in Mexico, the last to colonel. But when he had just become a major outside of Mexico City, 2nd Lt. Grant was finally able to shake loose the bonds of quartermaster and fight. At San Cosme, a Mexican artillery piece had stopped all movement down a key road. Grant led a column of volunteers around one flank, attacked, and drove them off in confusion. He then had a brilliant, if unusual, idea. Spying a church dominating a city square and a main gate, he had a mountain howitzer carried into the belfry. Once in place, its fire was devastating, and Mexicans forces fled yet again.

This action of Grant and the howitzer in the church belfry was mentioned in the official reports of General Worth, Colonel Garland, and Major Robert E. Lee. Though it is doubtful that Grant and Lee ever met in Mexico, it seems clear that they at least knew of each other. Lee was to distinguish himself once again in taking the heights of Chapultepec, where he was slightly wounded.

Lee and Grant both returned from Mexico in 1848. Grant married Julia on August 22, and they decided he should stay in the army for awhile. The Grants spent the next four years in New York and Michigan, a happy time of marital contentment. Then, in 1852, Grant was assigned to San Francisco, and they decided that Julia, expecting their second child, should wait to follow him west at a later point.

Grant's duties took him north to Vancouver, then to Humboldt Bay, close to San Francisco. And while he loved the West Coast, life in San Francisco was prohibitively expensive, and it was clear that he could not afford to keep his family there. It has often been charged that Grant had begun to drink too much, and that he had perhaps blown up at a superior officer who then threatened to court-martial him

unless he resigned. Whether that is true or not, or whatever role liquor may have played, is long beyond recovery. But in any case, Grant resigned his commission in 1854 and returned to Julia and his two sons near St. Louis.

Grant was eager to enter civilian life at first, and began farming land Julia had inherited. But after four unproductive years, he finally gave in, sold off his livestock and farm implements, and tried his hand in the real estate business. No better luck awaited him there, however, and he fell back on his family for support. In 1860, he was a salaried clerk working behind the counter in a leather goods store owned by his father in Galena, Illinois.

Life after Mexico had been quite different for Lee. When he returned home, his first assignment was to improve the defenses of Baltimore Harbor. Then, in September 1852, he took over as the ninth Superintendent at West Point. And while he had a strong influence on the academy, where he was the driving force behind numerous significant improvements, he was badly needed in the army. In 1855, he was assigned to the 2nd Cavalry in west Texas, which tried to protect civilian settlers from raids by Comanche Indians.

Lee returned to Arlington House periodically. On October 17, 1859, during one such trip, he received a visit from Lieutenant J.E.B. Stuart, who had been his son's classmate and close friend, and a good friend of the family while Lee was Superintendent. Stuart bore a note directing Lee to report to the Secretary of War. Lee was ordered to lead a detachment

RIGHT: Secession Hall in Charleston, South Carolina, birthplace of the Confederate States of America.

BELOW: Former South Carolina slaves at Hilton Head, liberated by the Federal occupation of 1861, sort cotton on a confiscated plantation.

of Marines to Harpers Ferry. And so it was that Lee, with Stuart at his side, commanded the force that captured John Brown, a man whose execution would long reverberate across America. This was the same John Brown who, in his youth, had shared a residence and friendship with Jesse Grant, the father of Ulysses.

After Lincoln's election in November 1860, southern states began to secede. General Winfield Scott told Lincoln that Lee was the finest officer in the US Army, and a week after Fort Sumter fell on April 13, Lincoln offered Lee the command of the Union army. He declined. Two days later, he went to Richmond, where command of the army of Virginia was offered to him. This offer he accepted. Although there are instances of officers going over to the enemy, it is unparalleled in history that a man would be offered the command of the two hostile armies.

After frustrating efforts to save the counties of Virginia that were to become the state of West Virginia, Lee was sent on a tour of the coastal defenses of South Carolina, Georgia, and Florida. As soon as he returned to Richmond, Jefferson Davis, the new President of the Confederate States of America, made him his chief military adviser.

When McClellan led the Union's Army of the Potomac on the Peninsular Campaign in 1862, it was Lee who organized the defenses of Richmond, and it was also Lee who was behind the brilliant diversion of sending General Thomas "Stonewall" Jackson storming through the Shenandoah Valley. On May 31, word got back to Richmond that General Joseph Johnston, commanding the resistance to McClellan, had been grievously wounded. Davis immediately sent Lee to replace Johnston, and thus fulfill his destiny as commander of the Army of Northern Virginia.

Grant, meanwhile, had been working as a civilian volunteer in the office of the governor of Illinois, helping to enlist regiments of volunteers. In 1861, General Winfield Scott, the commanding general of the US Army, had decided to keep the Regular Army units together and only supplement them with volunteer units drawn from the states. Grant refused service with these Illinois volunteers, and instead wrote to the Adjutant General of the US Army in Washington, offering to command a regiment in the Regular Army. But his offer was ignored.

As the call for more regiments came in, Grant wanted to join the fight. With the help of Congressman Elihu Washburn of Illinois, the governor of Illinois appointed Grant to command the 21st Illinois Volunteer Infantry Regiment, and he prepared to march off to war with his men.

Although Lee and Grant would become the commanders of the two main armies in the Civil War, they would not actually face each other on the battlefield until April 1864, after Grant had been promoted to Lieutenant General by Act of Congress and had become the Commanding General of the US Army. And while both men earned their spurs, so to speak, in the Mexican War, the lessons were quite different. Lee, as a senior captain on the commanding general's staff, filled a position that had a much higher profile, both politically and professionally. Grant, on the other hand, had graduated from West Point fourteen years after Lee, and as a junior officer was unable to avoid being detailed to the lowly position of quartermaster, from which few exploits demonstrating his personal courage or quick insight were expected or even possible. Still, lessons were learned in Mexico that had lasting impact on both men.

The excerpts from both memoirs that follow begin in early 1862. But 1861, the year when southern states seceded and Fort Sumter in Charleston Harbor was bombarded and taken by Confederate forces, was a crucial year. On July 21, 1861, Union forces were driven from the field in disorder at the Battle of Bull Run (Union designation) or First Manassas (Confederate) just south of

BUILT FROM THE RUINS.

the nation's capital in Washington D.C. Although this was the period in the Civil War when both sides were learning how and where and when to fight, both Lee and Grant began to establish a personal reputation of sorts. They became known by their military and political superiors, within the ranks of their respective armies, and, through newspaper accounts of their performance of their duties, in the minds of Americans living in both the North and the South. Before getting into the segments of the memoirs that follow, therefore, it is important for the reader to understand some of the earlier factors in the war that may have helped to shape them as the senior military leaders of each side. While Lee was by far the better-known and more widely respected figure to the public, as well as to military and governmental leaders, their early wartime careers almost seem to defy the differences in their ages and experience.

By July 1861, Grant felt that he had trained the 21st Illinois well enough to take the field, and soon enough, they had orders to attack a Confederate regiment commanded by

ABOVE: An engraving of the banner of South Carolina's convention of secession.

Ulysses S. Grant

Chapter I

Fort Henry and Fort Donelson

ort Henry occupies a bend in the river which gave the guns in the water battery a direct fire down the stream. The camp outside the fort was intrenched, with rifle pits and outworks two miles back on the road to Donelson and Dover. The garrison of the fort and camp was about 2,800, with strong reinforcements from Donelson halted some miles out. There were seventeen heavy guns in the fort. The river was very high, the banks being overflowed except where the bluffs come to the water's edge. A portion of the ground on which Fort Henry stood was two feet deep in water. Below, the water extended into the woods several hundred yards back from the bank on the east side. On the west bank Fort Heiman stood on high ground, completely

commanding Fort Henry. The distance from Fort Henry to Donelson is but eleven miles. The two positions were so important to the enemy, *as he saw his interest*, that it was natural to suppose that reinforcements would come from every quarter from which they could be got. Prompt action on our part was imperative.

The plan was for the troops and gunboats to start at the same moment. The troops were to invest the garrison and the gunboats to attack the fort at close quarters. General [Charles F.] Smith was to land a brigade of his division on the west bank during the night of the 5th and get it in rear of Heiman.

At the hour designated the troops and gunboats started. General Smith found Fort Heiman had been evacuated before his men

Grant as a Lieutenant general in 1864. His elevation to the highest military rank his country could confer was all but unimaginable two years earlier. It was the capture of forts Henry and Donelson that began his meteoric rise.

arrived. The gunboats soon engaged the water batteries at very close quarters, but the troops which were to invest Fort Henry were delayed for want of roads, as well as by the dense forest and the high water in what would in dry weather have been unimportant beds of streams. This delay made no difference in the result. On our first appearance [Confederate General Lloyd] Tilghman had sent his entire command, with the exception of about one hundred men left to man the guns in the fort, to the outworks on the road to Dover and Donelson, so as to have them out of range of the guns of our navy; and before any attack on the 6th he had ordered them to retreat on Donelson. He stated in his subsequent report that the defence was intended solely to give his troops time to make their escape.

Tilghman was captured with his staff and ninety men, as well as the armament of the fort, the ammunition and whatever stores were there. Our cavalry pursued the retreating column towards Donelson and picked up two guns and a few stragglers; but the enemy had so much the start, that the pursuing force did not get in sight of any except the stragglers.

All the gunboats engaged were hit many times. The damage, however, beyond what could be repaired by a small expenditure of money, was slight, except to the *Essex*. A shell penetrated the boiler of that vessel and exploded it, killing and wounding forty-eight men, nineteen of whom were soldiers who had been detailed to act with the navy. On several occasions during the war such details were made when the complement of men with the navy was insufficient for the duty before them. After the fall of Fort Henry Captain [S.L.] Phelps, commanding the iron-clad *Carondelet*, at my request ascended the Tennessee River and thoroughly destroyed the bridge of the Memphis and Ohio Railroad. . . .

On the 7th, the day after the fall of Fort Henry, I took my staff and the cavalry – a part of one regiment – and made a reconnoissance to within about a mile of the outer line of works at Donelson. I had known General [Gideon] Pillow in Mexico, and judged that with any force, no matter how small, I could march up to within gunshot of any intrenchments he was given to hold. I said this to the officers of my staff at the time. I knew that [John B.] Floyd was in command, but he was no soldier, and I judged that he would yield to Pillow's pretensions. I met, as I ex-

LEFT: Charles Ferguson Smith was probably Grant's ablest lieutenant in the assault on forts Henry and Donelson. He would die soon thereafter of an injury received at Shiloh.

BELOW: Confederate General Gideon Pillow was second in command at Fort Donelson. He amply confirmed Grant's low opinion of his abilities when Grant attacked the fort.

pected, no opposition in making the reconnoissance and, besides learning the topography of the country on the way and around Fort Donelson, found that there were two roads available for marching; one leading to the village of Dover, the other to Donelson.

Fort Donelson is two miles north, or down the river, from Dover. The fort, as it stood in 1861, embraced about one hundred acres of land. On the east it fronted the Cumberland; to the north it faced Hickman's creek, a small stream which at the time was deep and wide because of the back-water from the river; on the south was another small stream, or rather a ravine, opening into the Cumberland. This also was filled with backwater from the river. The fort stood on high ground, some of it as much as a hundred feet above the Cumberland. Strong protection to the heavy guns in the water batteries had been obtained by cutting away places for them in the bluff. To the west there was a line of rifle-pits some two miles back from the river at the farthest point. This line ran generally along the crest of high ground, but in one place crossed a ravine which opens into the river between the village and the fort. The ground inside and outside of this in-

LEFT: The U.S.S. *St. Louis* was the first of a series of ironclad river gunboats built for the Union navy by the engineer James Buchanan Eads. She was part of the squadron led by Andrew Hull Foote against Fort Donelson while Grant was attacking the place on land. Grant's respect for the Navy and readiness to work with it in combined operations was highly unusual among U.S. Army officers, and it would stand Grant in good stead in the Vicksburg Campaign.

PLAN OF
FORT DONELSON
AND ITS OUTWORKS
Surveyed under the direction of
Lieut.Col. J. B. McPHERSON, A.D.C.
and Captain of Engineers
BY
Lieuts. Jenney and Kossak.

Scale of Yards

—— Union
—— Confederate

EXPLANATIONS:

A WATER BATTERIES
   LOWER BATTERY 8 · 32-pdr guns
                 1 · 10 inch columbiad
   UPPER BATTERY 1 · 32-pdr heavy rifled gun
                 2 · 32-pdr carronades

B RIFLE-PITS carried by Gen. Smith's division

C GEN. GRANT'S Headqrs. during the siege

D PART OF ENEMY'S INTRENCHMENTS
   carried by portion of
   Gen. McClernand's Div.

✗ ✗ ✗ FALLEN TIMBER

▲▲▲▲ ENEMY'S TENTS

▦▦▦▦ ENEMY'S LOG HUTS

⌀⌀⌀ WOODS

SERIES 1 VOL 7 PAGE 164.

trenched line was very broken and generally wooded. The trees outside of the rifle-pits had been cut down for a considerable way out, and had been felled so that their tops lay outwards from the intrenchments. The limbs had been trimmed and pointed, and thus formed an abatis in front of the greater part of the line. Outside of this intrenched line, and extending about half the entire length of it, is a ravine running north and south and opening into Hickman creek at a point north of the fort. The entire side of this ravine next to the works was one long abatis. . . .

I was very impatient to get to Fort Donelson because I knew the importance of the place to the enemy and supposed he would reinforce it rapidly. I felt that 15,000 men on the 8th would be more effective than 50,000 a month later. I asked Flag-officer [Andrew] Foote, therefore, to order his gunboats still about Cairo to proceed up the Cumberland River and not to wait for those gone to Eastport and Florence; but the others got back in time and we started on the 12th. I had moved [General John A.] McClernand out a few miles the night before so as to leave the road as free as possible. . . .

ABOVE: A contemporary U.S. Army map shows the position of opposing forces during the investment of Fort Donelson.

OPPOSITE: John B. Floyd, the confederate commander of Fort Donelson. Grant's contempt for Pillow, Floyd's second in command, was mild compared to his feelings about Floyd.

along the crest of the ridges. The artillery was protected by being sunk in the ground. The men who were not serving the guns were perfectly covered from fire on taking position a little back from the crest. The greatest suffering was from want of shelter. It was midwinter and during the siege we had rain and snow, thawing and freezing alternately. It would not do to allow camp-fires except far down the hill out of sight of the enemy, and it would not do to allow many of the troops to remain there at the same time. In the march over from Fort Henry numbers of the men had thrown away their blankets and overcoats. There was . . . much discomfort and . . . suffering.

During the 12th and 13th, and until the arrival of [General Lewis] Wallace and [Colonel] Thayer on the 14th, the National forces, composed of but 15,000 men, without intrenchments, confronted an intrenched army of 21,000, without conflict further than what was brought on by ourselves. Only one gunboat had arrived. There was a little skirmishing each day, brought on by the movement of our troops in securing commanding positions; but there was no actual fighting during this time except once, on the 13th, in front of McClernand's command. That general had undertaken to capture a battery of the enemy which was annoying his men. Without orders or

ABOVE: Flag Officer Andrew Hull Foote, commander of the Navy's riverine flotilla and a staunch admirer and ally of General Grant.

RIGHT: General Lewis (Lew) Wallace, one of Grant's abler lieutenants at Donelson, later became famous as the author of the novel *Ben Hur*.

I started from Fort Henry with 15,000 men, including eight batteries and part of a regiment of cavalry, and, meeting with no obstruction to detain us, the advance arrived in front of the enemy by noon. That afternoon and the next day were spent in taking up ground to make the investment as complete as possible. . . . The troops were not intrenched, but the nature of the ground was such that they were just as well protected from the fire of the enemy as if rifle-pits had been thrown up. Our line was generally

ABOVE: The railway station at Corinth, Mississippi. Because Grant's superiors failed to follow up his victory over the river forts, the enemy was able to regroup in Corinth and mount the counterstroke that resulted in the Battle of Shiloh in early April.

LEFT: Bushrod R. Johnson was among the senior Confederate officers who escaped from Fort Donelson. He would clash with Grant again less than two months later at Shiloh.

Chapter II

Shiloh

The news of the fall of forts Henry and Donelson was received with delight in the victory-starved North and served to focus national attention for the first time on "Unconditional Surrender" Grant, who was promptly promoted to the grade of major-general. Grant was convinced – then, and to the end of his days – that if the capture of the two strategically-located river forts had quickly been followed up with a series of coordinated Federal strikes at Chattanooga, Corinth, Memphis, and Vicksburg, virtually all of the Confederacy west of the Alleghenies might have fallen to the Union in 1862. But such daring thinking was beyond the grasp of the plodding, ungracious Halleck. Instead, Halleck took no coherent action, set up a great clamor for reinforcements, and even found occasion to *pick a petty quarrel with Grant and to remove him – fortunately, only temporarily – from his command. In the meantime, the enemy was granted precious time to regroup his armies and to fortify new positions. By mid-March, when Grant was restored to his command of the District of Cairo, the Confederates had assembled a considerable army in Corinth, in northern Mississippi, under the command of the redoubtable Albert Sidney Johnston and his celebrated lieutenant P. G. T. Beauregard. It was against this force that Grant, whose troops were then centered on Savannah, in southern Tennessee, was now belatedly ordered to move. But Johnston moved even Faster: the result would be the bloodiest battle yet fought in the Western Hemisphere.*

W hen I reassumed command on the 17th of March I found the army divided, about half being on the east bank of the Tennessee at Savannah, while one division was at Crump's landing on the west bank about four miles higher up, and the remainder at Pittsburg landing, five miles above Crump's. The enemy was in force at Corinth, the junction of the two most important railroads in the Mississippi valley – one connecting Memphis and the Mississippi River with the East, and the other leading south to all the cotton states. Still another railroad connects Corinth with Jackson, in west Tennessee. If we obtained possession of Corinth the enemy would have no railroad for the transportation of armies or supplies until that running east from Vicksburg was reached. It was the great strategic position at the West between the Tennessee and the Mississippi rivers and between Nashville and Vicksburg.

I at once put all the troops at Savannah in motion for Pittsburg landing, knowing that the enemy was fortifying at Corinth and

collecting an army there under Johnston. It was my expectation to march against that army as soon as [General Don Carlos] Buell, who had been ordered to reinforce me with the Army of the Ohio, should arrive; and the west bank of the river was the place to start from. . . .

On the 17th of March the army on the Tennessee River consisted of five divisions, commanded respectively by Generals C. F. Smith, [J. A.] McClernand, L. Wallace, [S.] Hurlbut, and [W. T.] Sherman. General W. H. L. Wallace was temporarily in command of Smith's division, General Smith, as I have said, being confined to his bed. Reinforcements were arriving daily and as they came up they were organized, first into brigades, then into a division, and the command given to General [Benjamin] Prentiss, who had been ordered to report to me. General Buell was on his way from Nashville with 40,000 veterans. . . .

At this time I generally spent the day at Pittsburg and returned to Savannah in the evening. I was intending to remove my headquarters to Pittsburg, but Buell was expected daily and would come in at Savannah. I remained at this point, therefore, a few days longer than I otherwise should have done, in order to meet him on his arrival. The skirmishing in our front, however, had been so continuous from about the 3d of April that I did not leave Pittsburg each night until an hour when I felt there would be no further danger before the morning. . . .

On the 5th General [William] Nelson, with a division of Buell's army, arrived at Savannah and I ordered him to move up the east bank of the river, to be in a position where he could be ferried over to Crump's landing or Pittsburg as occasion required. I had learned that General Buell himself would be at Savannah the next day, and desired to meet me on his arrival. . . . While I was at breakfast, however, heavy firing was heard in the direction of Pittsburg landing, and I hastened there, sending a hurried note to Buell informing him of the reason why I could not meet him at Savannah.

Up to that time I had felt by no means certain that Crump's landing might not be the point of attack. On reaching the front, however, about eight A.M., I found that the attack on Pittsburg was unmistakable. . . .

Some two of three miles from Pittsburg landing was a log meeting-house called

OPPOSITE: William Tecumseh Sherman. During the siege of Fort Donelson, Sherman, even though Grant's superior in rank, had offered to place himself under Grant's orders. At Shiloh he proved to be, by far, Grant's most effective lieutenant. From this early association was born what was to become one of the greatest partnerships in the history of warfare.

BELOW: Union troops foraging for food. The troops in this scene happened to belong to the division commanded by Benjamin Prentiss, soon to be the hero of the "Hornet's Nest" at Shiloh.

thing was favorable to the Union side. We had now become the attacking party. The enemy was driven back all day, as we had been the day before, until finally he beat a precipitate retreat. The last point held by him was near the road leading from the landing to Corinth, on the left of Sherman and right of McClernand. About three o'clock, being near that point and seeing that the enemy was giving way everywhere else, I gathered up a couple of regiments, or parts of regiments, from troops near by, formed them in line of battle and marched them forward, going in front myself to prevent premature or long-range firing. At this point there was a clearing between us and the enemy favorable for charging, although exposed. I knew the enemy were ready to break and only wanted a little encouragement from us to go quickly and join their friends who had started earlier. After marching to within musket-range I stopped and let the troops pass. The command, *Charge*, was given, and was executed with loud cheers and with a run; when the last of the enemy broke.

* * *

Shiloh was the severest battle fought at the West during the war, and but few in the East equalled it for hard, determined fight-ing. I saw an open field, in our possession on the second day, over which the Confederates had made repeated charges the day before, so covered with dead that it would have been possible to walk across the clearing, in any direction, stepping on dead bodies, without a foot touching the ground. On our side National and Confederate troops were mingled together in about equal proportions; but on the remainder of the field nearly all were Confederates. On one

ABOVE: Union troops under General Rousseau's command recapture artillery that the Confederates had taken from them earlier in the battle.

THE BATTLE OF PITTSBURGH, TENN. APRIL 7TH 1862.

LEFT: This Currier and Ives print depicts Grant personally leading the cavalry charge that ended the fighting at Shiloh. Shiloh was a tactical "draw," but a strategic loss for the Confederate forces.

ABOVE: A patriotic engraving shows Grant leading an heroic charge at Shiloh. It does not much matter that the officer in question looks little like Grant, since there was never any such charge.

part, which had evidently not been ploughed for several years, probably because the land was poor, bushes had grown up, some to the height of eight or ten feet. There was not one of these left standing unpierced by bullets. The smaller ones were all cut down.

Contrary to all my experience up to that time, and to the experience of the army I was then commanding, we were on the defensive. We were without intrenchments or defensive advantages of any sort, and more than half the army engaged the first day was without experience or even drill as soldiers. The officers with them, except the division commanders and possibly two or three of the brigade commanders, were equally inexperienced in war. The result was a Union victory that gave the men who achieved it great confidence in themselves ever after.

The enemy fought bravely, but they had started out to defeat and destroy an army and capture a position. They failed in both, with very heavy loss in killed and wounded, and must have gone back discouraged and convinced that the "Yankee" was not an enemy to be despised. . . .

General Albert Sidney Johnston, who commanded the Confederate forces at the beginning of the battle, was disabled by a wound on the afternoon of the first day. This wound, as I understood afterwards, was not necessarily fatal, or even dangerous. But he was a man who would not abandon what he deemed an important trust in the face of danger and consequently continued in the saddle, commanding, until so exhausted by the loss of blood that he had to be taken from his horse, and soon after died. The

LEFT: Shiloh, with combined casualties of some 24,000, was the bloodiest battle fought so far in the Western Hemisphere. No photographs were taken of the dead but they would have looked exactly like these Confederates awaiting burial at Antietam.

RIGHT: When Albert Sidney Johnston received a mortal wound at Shiloh many in the South believed that the CSA had lost its greatest general. Grant, however, was never much impressed by the tactics that Johnston used at Shiloh.

news was not long in reaching our side and I suppose was quite an encouragement to the National soldiers.

I had known Johnston slightly in the Mexican war and later as an officer in the regular army. He was a man of high character and ability. His contemporaries at West Point, and officers generally who came to know him personally later and who remained on our side, expected him to prove the most formidable man to meet that the Confederacy would produce.

I once wrote that nothing occurred in his brief command of an army to prove or disprove the high estimate that had been placed upon his military ability; but after studying the orders and dispatches of Johnston I am compelled to materially modify my views of that officer's qualifications as a soldier. My judgment is now that he was vacillating and undecided in his actions. . . .

He knew the National troops were preparing to attack him in his chosen position. But he had evidently become so disturbed at the results of his operations that he resolved to strike out in an offensive campaign which would restore all that was lost, and if successful accomplish still more. . . . The design was a bold one; but . . . in the execution Johnston showed vacillation and indecision. He left Corinth on the 2d of April and was not ready to attack until the 6th. The distance his army had to march was less than twenty miles. [General P. G. T.] Beauregard, his second in command, was opposed to the attack for two reasons: first, he thought, if let alone the National troops would attack the Confederates in their intrenchments; second, we were in ground of our own choosing and would necessarily be intrenched. Johnston not only listened to the objection of Beauregard to an attack, but held a council of war on the subject on the morning of the 5th. On the evening of the same day he was in consultation with some of his generals on the same subject, and still again on the morning of the 6th. During this last consultation, and before a decision had been reached, the battle began by the National troops opening fire on the enemy. This seemed to settle the question as to whether there was to be any battle of Shiloh. It also seems to me to settle the question as to whether there was a surprise.

I do not question the personal courage of General Johnston, or his ability. But he did not win the distinction predicted for him by many of his friends. He did prove that as a general he was over-estimated.

General Beauregard was next in rank to Johnston and succeeded to the command, which he retained to the close of the battle and during the subsequent retreat on Corinth, as well as in the siege of that place. His tactics have been severely criticised by Confederate writers, but I do not believe his fallen chief could have done any better under the circumstances. Some of these critics claim that Shiloh was won when Johnston fell, and that if he had not fallen the army under me would have been annihilated or captured. *Ifs* defeated the Confederates at Shiloh. There is little doubt that we would have been disgracefully beaten *if* all the shells and bullets fired by us had passed harmlessly over the enemy and *if* all of theirs had taken effect. Commanding generals are liable to be killed during engagements; and the fact that when he was shot Johnston was leading a brigade to induce it to make a charge which had been repeatedly ordered, is evidence that there was neither the universal demoralization on our side nor the unbounded confidence on theirs which has been claimed. . . .

The endeavor of the enemy on the first day was simply to hurl their men against ours — first at one point, then at another, some-times at several points at once. This they did with daring and energy, until at night the rebel troops were worn out. Our effort during the same time was to be prepared to resist assaults wherever made. The object of the Confederates on the second day was to get away with as much of their army and material as possible. Ours then was to drive them from our front, and to capture or destroy as great a part as possible of their men and material. We were successful in driving them back, but not so successful in captures as if farther pursuit could have been made. As it was, we captured or recaptured on the second day about as much artillery as we lost on the first; and, leaving out the one great capture of Prentiss, we took more prisoners on Monday than the enemy gained from us on Sunday. . . .

Our loss in the two days' fight was 1,754 killed, 8,408 wounded and 2,885 missing. Of these, 2,103 were in the Army of the Ohio. Beauregard reported a total loss of 10,699, of whom 1,728 were killed, 8,012 wounded and 957 missing. This estimate must be incorrect. We buried, by actual count, more of the

BELOW: William Bate was still serving as an enlisted man in a Tennessee regiment when he was wounded at Shiloh. By the war's end he would be a Confederate major general.

mysterious movements were aroused. Our river guards discovered one day a small skiff moving quietly and mysteriously up the river near the east shore, from the direction of Vicksburg, towards the fleet. On overhauling the boat they found a small white flag, not much larger than a handkerchief, set up in the stern, no doubt intended as a flag of truce in case of discovery. The boat, crew and passengers were brought ashore to me. The chief personage aboard proved to be Jacob Thompson, Secretary of the Interior under the administration of President Buchanan. After a pleasant conversation of half an hour or more I allowed the boat and crew, passengers and all, to return to Vicksburg, without creating a suspicion that there was a doubt in my mind as to the good faith of Mr. Thompson and his flag.

Admiral Porter proceeded with the preparation of the steamers for their hazardous passage of the enemy's batteries. The great essential was to protect the boilers from the enemy's shot, and to conceal the fires under the boilers from view. This he accomplished by loading the steamers, between the guards and boilers on the boiler deck up to the deck

ABOVE: Flag Officer David Dixon Porter's Mississippi Squadron makes its daring run past the big guns of the Vicksburg batteries on the night of April 16, 1863. The ships were under heavy fire for over two hours, but only one, a transport, was lost.

RIGHT: David Dixon Porter. For his contribution to the success of Grant's Vicksburg Campaign, Porter was rewarded by a promotion that jumped him two grades in permanent rank to a rear admiralcy.

above, with bales of hay and cotton, and the deck in front of the boilers in the same way, adding sacks of grain. The hay and grain would be wanted below, and could not be transported in sufficient quantity by the muddy roads over which we expected to march.

Before this I had been collecting, from St. Louis and Chicago, yawls and barges to be used as ferries when we got below. By the 16th of April Porter was ready to start on his perilous trip. The advance, flagship *Benton*, Porter commanding, started at ten o'clock at night, followed at intervals of a few minutes by the *Lafayette* with a captured steamer, the *Price*, lashed to her side, the *Louisville*, *Mound City, Pittsburgh* and *Carondelet* – all of these being naval vessels. Next came the transports – *Forest Queen, Silver Wave* and *Henry Clay*, each towing barges loaded with coal to be used as fuel by the naval and transport steamers when below the batteries. The gunboat *Tuscumbia* brought up the rear. Soon after the start a battery between Vicksburg and Warrenton opened fire across the intervening peninsula, followed by the upper batteries, and then by batteries all along the line. The gunboats ran up close under the bluffs, delivering their fire in return at short distances, probably without much effect. They were under fire for more than two hours and every vessel was struck many times, but with little damage to the gunboats. The transports did not fare so well. The *Henry Clay* was disabled and deserted by her crew. Soon after a shell burst in the cotton packed about the boilers, set the vessel on fire and burned her to the water's edge. The burning mass, however, floated down to Carthage before grounding, as did also one of the barges in tow.

The enemy were evidently expecting our fleet, for they were ready to light up the river by means of bonfires on the east side and by firing houses on the point of land opposite the city on the Louisiana side. The sight was magnificent, but terrible. I witnessed it from the deck of a river transport, run out into the middle of the river and as low down as it was prudent to go. My mind was much relieved when I learned that no one on the transports had been killed and but few, if any, wounded. During the running of the batteries men were stationed in the holds of the transports to partially stop with cotton shot-holes that might be made in the hulls. All damage was afterwards soon repaired under the direction of Admiral Porter. . . .

Once Porter's squadron was below Vicksburg, Grant set his army in motion. While Sherman made a demonstration north of Vicksburg, McClernand's and McPherson's corps moved south along the Louisiana shore, sometimes marching and sometimes ferried in Porter's transports, until they reached a point a little south of the Confederate stronghold Grand Gulf.

When the troops debarked, the evening of the 29th, it was expected that we would have to go to Rodney, about nine miles below, to find a landing; but that night a colored man came in who informed me that a good landing would be found at Bruinsburg, a few miles above Rodney, from which point there was a good road leading to Port Gibson some twelve miles in the interior. The information was found correct, and our landing was effected without opposition.

Sherman had not left his position above Vicksburg yet. On the morning of the 27th I ordered him to create a diversion by moving his corps up the Yazoo and threatening an attack on Haines' Bluff.

My object was to compel Pemberton to keep as much force about Vicksburg as I could, until I could secure a good footing on high land east of the river. The move was eminently successful and, as we afterwards learned, created great confusion about Vicksburg and doubts about our real design. Sherman moved the day of our attack on Grand Gulf, the 29th, with ten regiments of his command and eight gunboats which Porter had left above Vicksburg.

He debarked his troops and apparently

BELOW: River steamers unload supplies at Young's Point, Grant's headquarters above Vicksburg, in March 1863.

ABOVE: The Confederates had no monopoly on artillery in the Vicksburg Campaign. Here, a Union battery composed of mixed siege and field guns.

OPPOSITE TOP: Some of the larger houses in Vicksburg. The house in the foreground would be taken over by the U.S. Army Signal Corps after the city's capture.

OPPOSITE BOTTOM: General John A. Logan (fifth from right) was an excellent divisional commander in McPherson's corps. He was given a corps command of his own at the end of the Vicksburg Campaign.

made every preparation to attack the enemy while the navy bombarded the main forts at Haines' Bluff. This move was made without a single casualty in either branch of the service. On the first of May Sherman received orders from me (sent from Hard Times the evening of the 29th of April) to withdraw from the front of Haines' Bluff and follow McPherson with two divisions as fast as he could.

I had established a depot of supplies at Perkins' plantation. Now that all our gunboats were below Grand Gulf it was possible that the enemy might fit out boats in the Big Black with improvised armament and attempt to destroy these supplies. McPherson was at Hard Times with a portion of his corps, and the depot was protected by a part of his command. The night of the 29th I directed him to arm one of the transports with artillery and send it up to Perkins' plantation as a guard; and also to have the siege guns we had brought along moved there and put in position.

The embarkation below Grand Gulf took place at De Shroon's, Louisiana, six miles above Bruinsburg, Mississippi. Early on the morning of 30th of April McClernand's corps

and one division of McPherson's corps were speedily landed.

When this was effected I felt a degree of relief scarcely ever equalled since. Vicksburg was not yet taken it is true, nor were its defenders demoralized by any of our previous moves. I was now in the enemy's country, with a vast river and the stronghold of Vicksburg between me and my base of supplies. But I was on dry ground on the same side of the river with the enemy. All the campaigns, labors, hardships and exposures from the month of December previous to this time that had been made and endured, were for . . . this one object.

I had with me the 13th corps, General McClernand commanding, and two brigades of [John A.] Logan's division of the 17th corps, General McPherson commanding – in all not more than twenty thousand men to commence the campaign with. These were soon reinforced by the remaining brigade of Logan's division and [M.M.] Crocker's division of the 17th corps. On the 7th of May I was further reinforced by Sherman with two divisions of his, the 15th corps. My total force was then about thirty-three thousand men.

OPPOSITE TOP: A U.S. Army map of the theater of Grant's brilliant Vicksburg Campaign. In 18 days after crossing the Mississippi he would march 200 miles, win every battle, and divide and outwit Rebel forces larger than his own – all behind enemy lines.

OPPOSITE BOTTOM: John Logan as a major general. After the war he would represent the state of Illinois in the U.S. House of Representatives and the Senate for two decades.

BELOW: A famous Mathew Brady photograph of Ulysses S. Grant in the field.

The enemy occupied Grand Gulf, Haines' Bluff and Jackson with a force of nearly sixty thousand men. Jackson is fifty miles east of Vicksburg and is connected with it by a railroad. My first problem was to capture Grand Gulf to use as a base. . . .

The key to the taking of Grand Gulf was the capture of strategically-located Port Gibson, 12 miles inland. Both the Grand Gulf garrison and Grant's troops raced toward Port Gibson, clashed there, and the Union prevailed. During the night of May 2 the Confederates evacuated Grand Gulf.

When I reached Grand Gulf May 3rd I had not been with my baggage since the 27th of April and consequently had had no change of underclothing, no meal except such as I could pick up sometimes at other headquarters, and no tent to cover me. The first thing I did was to get a bath, borrow some fresh underclothing from one of the naval officers and get a good meal on the flagship. Then I wrote letters to the general-in-chief informing him of our present position, dispatches to be telegraphed from Cairo, orders to General [J. C.] Sullivan commanding above Vicksburg, and gave orders to all my corps commanders. About twelve o'clock at night I was through my work and

started for Hankinson's ferry, arriving there before daylight. While at Grand Gulf I heard from [Nathaniel] Banks, who was on the Red River, and who said that he could not be at Port Hudson before the 10th of May and then with only 15,000 men. Up to this time my intention had been to secure Grand Gulf, as a base of supplies, detach McClernand's corps to Banks and co-operate with him in the reduction of Port Hudson.

The news from Banks forced upon me a different plan of campaign from the one intended. To wait for his co-operation would have detained me at least a month. The reinforcements would not have reached ten thousand men after deducting casualties and necessary river guards at all high points close to the river for over three hundred miles. The enemy would have strengthened his position and been reinforced by more men than Banks could have brought. I therefore determined to move independently of Banks, cut loose from my base, destroy the rebel force in rear of Vicksburg and invest or capture the city.

Grand Gulf was accordingly given up as a base and the authorities at Washington were notified. I knew well that Halleck's caution would lead him to disapprove of this course; but it was the only one that gave any chance of success. The time it would take to communicate with Washington and get a reply would be so great that I could not be interfered with until it was demonstrated whether my plan was practicable. Even Sherman, who afterwards ignored bases of supplies other than what were afforded by the country while marching through four States of the Confederacy with an army more than twice as large as mine at this time, wrote me from Hankinson's ferry, advising me of the impossibility of supplying our army over a single road. He urged me to "stop all troops till your army is partially supplied with wagons, and then act as quick as possible; for this road will be jammed, as sure as life." To this I replied: "I do not calculate upon the possibility of supplying the army with full rations from Grand Gulf. I know it will be impossible without constructing additional roads. What I do expect is to get up what rations of hard bread, coffee and salt we can, and make the country furnish the balance." . . .

Up to this point our movements had been made without serious opposition. My line was now nearly parallel with the Jackson and Vicksburg railroad and about seven

MAP
OF THE
COUNTRY
BETWEEN
VICKSBURG AND MERIDIAN, MISS.
SHOWING THE
ROUTE FOLLOWED
BY THE
SEVENTEENTH ARMY CORPS
under the command of
MAJ. GEN. J.B. MᶜPHERSON
in February, 1864.
Surveyed by
Lᵗˢ H.M. BUSH and Assistants S. DAVIS and S.W. DUNNING
under the direction of
CAPᵗ A. HICKENLOOPER, Chf. Engᵣ
Scale.

LEGEND
Route of 16ᵗʰ and 17ᵗʰ Corps
Route of Seventeenth Corps
Route of Sixteenth Corps
Confederate

miles south of it. The right was at Raymond eighteen miles from Jackson, McPherson commanding; Sherman was in the centre on Fourteen Mile Creek, his advance thrown across; McClernand to the left, also on Fourteen Mile Creek, advance across, and his pickets within two miles of Edward's station, where the enemy had concentrated a considerable force and where they undoubtedly expected us to attack. McClernand's left was on the Big Black. In all our moves, up to this time, the left had hugged the Big Black closely, and all the ferries had been guarded to prevent the enemy throwing a force on our rear.

McPherson encountered the enemy, five thousand strong with two batteries under General [J.] Gregg, about two miles out of Raymond. This was about two P.M. Logan was in advance with one of his brigades. He deployed and moved up to engage the enemy. McPherson ordered the road in rear to be cleared of wagons, and the balance of Logan's division, and Crocker's, which was still farther in rear, to come forward with all dispatch. The order was obeyed with alacrity. Logan got his division in position for assault before Crocker could get up, and attacked with vigor, carrying the enemy's position easily, sending Gregg flying from the field not to appear against our front again until we met at Jackson.

In this battle McPherson lost 66 killed, 339 wounded, and 37 missing – nearly or not quite all from Logan's division. The enemy's loss was 100 killed, 305 wounded, besides 415 taken prisoners. . . .

When the news reached me of McPherson's victory at Raymond about sundown my position was with Sherman. I decided at once to turn the whole column towards Jackson and capture that place without delay.

Pemberton was now on my left, with, as I supposed, about 18,000 men; in fact, as I learned afterwards, with nearly 50,000. A force was also collecting on my right, at Jackson, the point where all the railroads communicating with Vicksburg connect. All the enemy's supplies of men and stores would come by that point. As I hoped in the end to besiege Vicksburg, I must first destroy all possibility of aid. I therefore determined to move swiftly towards Jackson, destroy or drive any force in that direction and then turn upon Pemberton. But by moving against Jackson, I uncovered my own communication. So I finally decided to have none – to cut loose altogether from my base and move my whole force eastward. I then had no fears for my communications, and if I moved quickly enough could turn upon Pemberton before he could attack me in the rear. . . .

General Joseph E. Johnston arrived at Jackson in the night of the 13th from Tennessee, and immediately assumed command of all the Confederate troops in Mississippi. I knew he was expecting reinforcements from the south and east. . . .

I notified General Halleck that I should attack the State capital on the 14th. A courier carried the dispatch to Grand Gulf through an unprotected country.

Sherman and McPherson communicated with each other during the night and arranged to reach Jackson at about the same hour. It rained in torrents during the night of the 13th and the fore part of the day of the 14th. The roads were intolerable, and in some places on Sherman's line, where the land was low, they were covered more than a foot deep with water. But the troops never murmured. By nine o'clock Crocker, of McPherson's corps, who was now in advance, came upon the enemy's pickets and speedily drove them in upon the main body. They were outside of the intrenchments in a strong position, and proved to be which there is a railroad tunnel, intervenes between the two hills. The problem now was to get to the main ridge. The enemy was fortified on the point; and back farther, where the ground was still higher, was a second fortification commanding the first. Sherman was out as soon as it was light enough to see, and by sunrise his command was in motion. Three brigades held the hill already gained. Morgan L. Smith moved along the east base of Missionary Ridge; [G.] Loomis along the west base, supported by two brigades of John E. Smith's division; and [J.M.] Corse with his brigade was between the two, moving directly towards the hill to be captured. The ridge is steep and heavily wooded on the east side, where M. L. Smith's troops were advancing, but cleared and with a more gentle slope on the west side. The troops advanced rapidly and carried the extreme end of the rebel works. Morgan L. Smith advanced to a point which cut the enemy off from the railroad bridge and the means of bringing up supplies by rail from Chickamauga Station, where the main depot was located. The enemy made brave and strenuous efforts to drive our troops from the position we had gained, but without suc-

cess. The contest lasted for two hours. Corse, a brave and efficient commander, was badly wounded in this assault. Sherman now threatened both Bragg's flanks and his stores, and made it necessary for him to weaken other points of his line to strengthen his right. From the position I occupied I could see column after column of Bragg's forces moving against Sherman. Every Confederate gun that could be brought to bear upon the Union forces was concentrated upon him. . . . This was what I wanted. But it had now got to be late in the afternoon, and I had expected before this to see Hooker crossing the ridge in the neighborhood of Rossville and compelling Bragg to mass in that direction also.

The enemy had evacuated Lookout Mountain during the night, as I expected he would. In crossing the valley he burned the bridge over Chattanooga Creek, and did all he could to obstruct the roads behind him. Hooker was off bright and early, with no obstructions in his front but distance and the destruction above named. He was detained four hours crossing Chattanooga Creek, and thus was lost the immediate advantage I expected from his forces. His reaching Bragg's

ABOVE: Lookout Mountain, as viewed from the Tennessee. It was Hooker's assignment to take the mountain on November 24. He did so but was then dilatory in repositioning his troops to join in the main attack on Missionary Ridge the next day.

RIGHT: A view of Chattanooga looking southwest toward Lookout Mountain.

OPPOSITE: The Union charge up Missionary Ridge.

OPPOSITE BOTTOM: The landing from which the Union forces in Chattanooga received most of their supplies.

BELOW: A Union map of the Chattanooga battle area.

MAP
ACCOMPANYING REPORT
OF
MAJ. GEN. O.O. HOWARD.

ABOVE: A photograph taken after the battle shows well the terrain the Union army had to cross in attacking Missionary Ridge.

RIGHT: Among the Confederate victors at Chickamauga was Montgomery Dent Corse, who led the brigade that George Pickett had once commanded.

OPPOSITE TOP: After Rebel forces were expelled from the Chattanooga area Union engineers built this bridge over the Tennessee.

flank and extending across it was to be the signal for Thomas's assault of the ridge. But Sherman's condition was getting so critical that the assault for his relief could not be delayed any longer.

[Philip] Sheridan's and [Thomas] Wood's divisions had been lying under arms from early morning, ready to move the instant the signal was given. I now directed Thomas to order the charge at once. a.. [I]n an incredibly short time loud cheering was heard, and [Wood] and Sheridan were driving the enemy's advance before them towards Missionary Ridge. The Confederates were strongly intrenched on the crest of the ridge in front of us, and had a second line half-way down and another at the base. Our men drove the troops in front of the lower line of rifle-pits so rapidly, and followed them so closely, that rebel and Union troops went over the first line of works almost at the same time. Many rebels were captured and sent to the rear under the fire of their own friends higher up the hill. Those that were not captured retreated, and were pursued. The retreating hordes being between friends and pursuers caused the enemy to fire high to avoid killing their own men. In fact, on that occasion the Union soldier nearest the enemy was in the safest position. Without awaiting further orders or stopping to re-form, on our troops went to the second line of works; over that and on for the crest – thus effectually carrying out my orders of the 18th for the battle and of the 24th for his charge.

I watched their progress with intense interest. The fire along the rebel line was terrific. Cannon and musket balls filled the air: but the damage done was in small proportion to the ammunition expended. The pursuit continued until the crest was reached, and soon our men were seen climbing over the Confederate barriers at different points in front of both Sheridan's and Wood's divisions. The retreat of the enemy along most of his line was precipitate and the panic so great that Bragg and his officers lost all control over their men. Many were captured, and thousands threw away their arms in their flight. . . .

The victory at Chattanooga was won against great odds, considering the advantage the enemy had of position, and was accomplished more easily than was expected by reason of Bragg's making several grave mistakes: first, in sending away his

ablest corps commander with over twenty thousand troops; second, in sending away a division of troops on the eve of battle; third, in placing so much of a force on the plain in front of his impregnable position.

It was known that Mr. Jefferson Davis had visited Bragg on Missionary Ridge a short time before my reaching Chattanooga. It was reported and believed that he had come out to reconcile a serious difference be-

ABOVE: The small frame house in Chattanooga where Sherman made his headquarters during the siege of the city.

I believed then, and see no reason to change that opinion now, that if the country had been such that Hancock and his command could have seen the confusion and panic in the lines of the enemy, it would have been taken advantage of so effectually that Lee would not have made another stand outside of his Richmond defences. . . .

Hancock followed Hill's retreating forces, in the morning, a mile or more. He maintained this position until, along in the afternoon, Longstreet came upon him. The retreating column of Hill meeting reinforcements that had not yet been engaged, became encouraged and returned with them. They were enabled, from the density of the forest, to approach within a few hundred yards of our advance before being discovered. Falling upon a brigade of Hancock's corps thrown to the advance, they swept it away almost instantly. The enemy followed up his advantage and soon came upon [Gershom] Mott's division, which fell back in great confusion. Hancock made dispositions to hold his advanced position, but after holding it for a time, fell back into the position that he had held in the morning, which was strongly intrenched. In this engagement the intrepid Wadsworth while trying to rally his men was mortally

BELOW: Union General Horatio Gouverneur Wright led VI Corps from the Wilderness through to Appomattox.

ABOVE: A pause in the fighting to celebrate St. Patrick's Day, March 17, 1863, in the Army of the Potomac with horse racing by General Thomas Meagher's Irish Brigade.

OPPOSITE TOP: Union cavalry General George A. Custer (right foreground) in 1861, when he was a lieutenant.

OPPOSITE: An Alfred R. Waud sketch of Grant writing out a telegraph message during the 1864 campaign.

wounded and fell into the hands of the enemy. The enemy followed up, but made no immediate attack.

The Confederate General [Micah] Jenkins was killed and Longstreet seriously wounded in this engagement. Longstreet had to leave the field, not to resume command for many weeks. His loss was a severe one to Lee, and compensated in a great measure for the mishap, or misapprehensions, which had fallen to our lot during the day. . . .

At 4:15 in the afternoon Lee attacked our left. His line moved up to within a hundred yards of ours and opened a heavy fire. This status was maintained for about half an hour. Then a part of Mott's division and [J. H. H.] Ward's brigade of [David] Birney's division gave way and retired in disorder. The enemy under R. H. Anderson took advan-

tage of this and pushed through our line, planting their flags on a part of the intrenchments not on fire. But owing to the efforts of Hancock, their success was but temporary. [Samuel] Carroll, of [John] Gibbon's division, moved at a double quick with his brigade and drove back the enemy, inflicting great loss. Fighting had continued from five in the morning sometimes along the whole line, at other times only in places. The ground fought over had varied in width, but averaged three-quarters of a mile. The killed, and many of the severely wounded, of both armies, lay within this belt where it was impossible to reach them. The woods were set on fire by the bursting shells, and the conflagration raged. The wounded who had not strength to move themselves were either suffocated or burned to death. Finally the fire communicated with our breastworks, in places. Being constructed of wood, they burned with great fury. But the battle still raged, our men firing through the flames until it became too hot to remain longer. . . .

During the night all of Lee's army withdrew within their intrenchments. On the morning of the 7th General [George A.] Custer drove the enemy's cavalry from Catharpin Furnace to Todd's Tavern. Pickets and skirmishers were sent along our entire front to find the position of the enemy. Some went as far as a mile and a half before finding him. But Lee showed no disposition to come out of his works. There was no battle during the day, and but little firing except in Warren's front; he being directed about noon to make reconnoissance in force. This drew some sharp firing, but there was no attempt on the part of Lee to drive him back. This ended the Battle of the Wilderness. . . .

ABOVE: An artist's somewhat romantic version of Grant leading his troops in the fruitless and costly Battle of Spottsylvania Court House, which took place soon after the Battle of the Wilderness.

More desperate fighting has not been witnessed on this continent than that of the 5th and 6th of May. Our victory consisted in having successfully crossed a formidable stream, almost in the face of an enemy, and in getting the army together as a unit. We gained an advantage on the morning of the 6th, which, if it had been followed up, must have proven very decisive. In the evening the enemy gained an advantage; but was speedily repulsed. As we stood at the close, the two armies were relatively in about the same condition to meet each other as when the river divided them. But the fact of having safely crossed was a victory.

Our losses in the Wilderness were very severe. Those of the Confederates must have been even more so; but I have no means of speaking with accuracy upon this point. The Germania Ford bridge was transferred to Ely's Ford to facilitate the transportation of the wounded to Washington. . . .

The Battle of the Wilderness set the pattern for the nightmarish campaign that was to follow. In two days of inconclusive fighting the North had lost 2,246 killed and 12,073 wounded, but Grant was determined not to let up the pressure on the enemy and quickly ordered a flanking movement around Lee's right wing to bring the Union army to Spottsylvania Court House. Lee anticipated the tactic, moved his forces accordingly, and was entrenched in Spottsylvania when Grant arrived. Grant attacked on May 12, made only token headway, and suffered 6800 more casualties. Again Grant wheeled his army to the left around Lee's flank, and again Lee countermaneuvered so as to block Grant's advance on the North Anna River. There followed another stalemated battle, another Union slide to the left, and now the two armies faced one another again at Cold Harbor.

The night of [May] 30th Lee's position was substantially from Atlee's Station on the Virginia Central Railroad south and east to the vicinity of Cold Harbor. Ours was: The left of Warren's corps was on the Shady Grove Road, extending to the Mechanicsville Road and about three miles south of the Totopoto-

LEFT: A rather misleading idea of the kind of terrain on which most of the Battle of the Wilderness was fought is projected in this popular Currier & Ives print.

BELOW: A U.S. Army map shows the general positions of the two armies in the Battle of the Wilderness and gives as well a good impression of how densely wooded the area was.

RIGHT: By 1864 railroads had become crucial instruments of war, not only for the rapid movement of men and supplies but also as platforms for mobile artillery. This big 32-lb Confederate rail gun, complete with a protective mantlet, is typical of the new forms of artillery that appeared during the last two years of the Civil War. This particular gun was used at Petersburg and perhaps even earlier in the 1864 campaign.

moy. Burnside to his right, then Hancock, and [H. G.] Wright on the extreme right, extending towards Hanover Court House, six miles south-east of it. Sheridan with two divisions of cavalry was watching our left front towards Cold Harbor. Wilson with his division on our right was sent to get on the Virginia Central Railroad and destroy it as far back as possible. He got possession of Hanover Court House the next day after a skirmish with [P. M. B.] Young's cavalry brigade. The enemy attacked Sheridan's pickets, but reinforcements were sent up and the attack was speedily repulsed and the enemy followed some distance towards Cold Harbor. . . .

On the 31st Sheridan advanced to near Old Cold Harbor. He found it intrenched and occupied by cavalry and infantry. A hard fight ensued but the place was carried. The enemy well knew the importance of Cold Harbor to us, and seemed determined that we should not hold it. He returned with such a large force that Sheridan was about withdrawing without making any effort to hold it against such odds; but about the time he commenced the evacuation he received orders to hold the place at all hazards, until reinforcements could be sent to him. He speedily turned the rebel works to face against them and placed his men in position for defence. Night came on before the enemy was ready for assault.

Wright's corps was ordered early in the evening to march directly to Cold Harbor passing by the rear of the army. It was expected to arrive by daylight or before; but the night was dark and the distance great, so that it was nine o'clock the 1st of June before it reached its destination. Before the arrival of Wright the enemy had made two assaults on Sheridan, both of which were repulsed with heavy loss to the enemy. Wright's corps coming up, there was no further assault on Cold Harbor.

[Corps Commander General William F.] Smith, who was coming up from White House, was also directed to march directly to Cold Harbor, and was expected early on the morning of the 1st of June; but by some blunder the order which reached Smith directed him to Newcastle instead of Cold Harbor. Through this blunder Smith did not reach his destination until three o'clock in the afternoon, and then with tired and worn-out men from their long and dusty march. He landed twelve thousand five hundred men from [Benjamin] Butler's command,

BELOW: At a conference held outside Bethesda Church on June 2 Grant leans over the shoulder of General George Meade to consult his map. The disastrous climax of the Battle of Cold Harbor would take place on the following day.

OPPOSITE TOP: The Battle of Cold Harbor according to Kurz & Allison. Grant regretted for the rest of his life the charge he ordered on June 3 against Lee's well-fortified position, for the charge proved to be an extremely costly failure.

OPPOSITE BOTTOM: Grant made up for his mistake at Cold Harbor in his next maneuver, a brilliant end-run that put him well to the south of Lee. The lower picture shows Grant's men crossing the Pamunkey River en route to the James.

but a division was left at White House temporarily and many men had fallen out of ranks in their long march.

Before the removal of Wright's corps from our right, after dark on the 31st, the two lines, Federal and Confederate, were so close together at that point that either side could detect directly any movement made by the other. Finding at daylight that Wright had left his front, Lee evidently divined that he had gone to our left. At all events, soon after light on the 1st of June [R. H.] Anderson, who commanded the corps on Lee's left, was seen moving along Warren's front. Warren was ordered to attack him vigorously in

GRANT'S GREAT CAMPAIGN—GENERAL BARLOW IN FRONT OF THE REBEL WORKS, TWELVE MILES FROM RICHMOND.—From a Sketch by A. R. Waud.—[See Page 410.]

flank, while Wright was directed to move out and get on his front. Warren fired his artillery at the enemy; but lost so much time in making ready that the enemy got by, and at three o'clock he reported the enemy was strongly intrenched in his front, and besides his lines were so long that he had no mass of troops to move with. He seemed to have forgotten that lines in rear of an army hold themselves while their defenders are fighting in their front. Wright reconnoitered some distance to his front: but the enemy finding Old Cold Harbor already taken had halted and fortified some distance west.

By six o'clock in the afternoon Wright and Smith were ready to make an assault. In front of both the ground was clear for several hundred yards, and then became wooded. Both charged across this open space and into the wood, capturing and holding the first line of rifle-pits of the enemy, and also capturing seven or eight hundred prisoners.

While this was going on, the enemy charged Warren three separate times with vigor, but were repulsed each time with loss. There was no officer more capable, nor one more prompt in acting, than Warren when the enemy forced him to it. There was also an attack upon Hancock's and Burnside's corps at the same time; but it was feeble and probably only intended to relieve Anderson who was being pressed by Wright and Smith.

During the night the enemy made frequent attacks with the view of dispossessing us of the important position we had gained, but without effecting their object.

Hancock was moved from his place in line during the night and ordered to the left of Wright. I expected to take the offensive on the morning of the 2d, but the night was so

BELOW: At his headquarters at City Point, on the James, Grant is visited by his wife and youngest son.

dark, the heat and dust so excessive and the roads so intricate and hard to keep, that the head of column only reached Old Cold Harbor at six o'clock, but was in position at 7:30 A.M. Preparations were made for an attack in the afternoon, but did not take place until the next morning. Warren's corps was moved to the left to connect with Smith: Hancock's corps was got into position to the left of Wright's, and Burnside was moved to Bethesda Church in reserve. While Warren and Burnside were making these changes the enemy came out several times and attacked them, capturing several hundred prisoners. The attacks were repulsed, but not followed up as they should have been. I was so annoyed at this that I directed Meade to instruct his corps commanders that they should seize all such opportunities when they occurred, and not wait for orders, all of our manoeuvres being made for the very purpose of getting the enemy out of his cover.

On this day [J. H.] Wilson returned from his raid upon the Virginia Central Railroad, having damaged it considerably. But, like ourselves, the rebels had become experts in repairing such damage. Sherman, in his memoirs, relates an anecdote of his campaign to Atlanta that well illustrates this point. The rebel cavalry lurking in his rear to burn bridges and obstruct his communications had become so disgusted at hearing trains go whistling by within a few hours after a bridge had been burned, that they proposed to try blowing up some of the tunnels. One of them said, "No use, boys, Old Sherman carries duplicate tunnels with him, and will replace them as fast as you can blow them up; better save your powder."

BELOW: An almost certainly forged picture purporting to be of Grant at City Point.

completion. The position of the two lines at
that point were only about a hundred yards
apart with a comparatively deep ravine intervening. In the bottom of this ravine the work
commenced. The position was unfavorable
in this particular: that the enemy's line at
that point was re-entering, so that its front
was commanded by their own lines both to
the right and left. Then, too, the ground was
sloping upward back of the Confederate line
for a considerable distance, and it was pre-
sumable that the enemy had, at least, a
detached work on this highest point. The
work progressed, and on the 23rd of July the
mine was finished ready for charging; but I
had this work of charging deferred until we
were ready for it.

On the 17th of July several deserters came
in and said that there was great consternation in Richmond, and that Lee was coming
out to make an attack upon us – the object
being to put us on the defensive so that he
might detach troops to go to Georgia where
the army Sherman was operating against
was said to be in great trouble. I put the army

ABOVE: General George Meade. As commander of the Army of the Potomac he was Grant's immediate subordinate during the Virginia campaigns of 1864-65, a trying position for a man as temperamental as Meade. Yet he seems to have handled the assignment capably and, on the whole, rather gracefully.

commanders, Meade and Butler, on the lookout, but the attack was not made.

I concluded, then, a few days later, to do something in the way of offensive movement myself, having in view something of the same object that Lee had had. [Horatio] Wright's and [William] Emory's corps were in Washington, and with this reduction of my force Lee might very readily have spared some troops from the defences to send West. I had other objects in view, however, besides keeping Lee where he was. The mine was constructed and ready to be exploded, and I wanted to take that occasion to carry Petersburg if I could. It was the object, therefore, to get as many of Lee's troops away from the south side of the James River as possible. Accordingly, on the 26th, we commenced a movement with Hancock's corps and Sheridan's cavalry to the north side by the way of Deep Bottom, where Butler had a pontoon bridge laid. The plan, in the main, was to let the cavalry cut loose and, joining with Kautz's cavalry of the Army of the James, get by Lee's lines and destroy as much as they could of the Virginia Central Railroad, while, in the mean time, the infantry was to move out so as to protect their rear and cover their retreat back when they should have got through with their work. We were successful in drawing the enemy's troops to the north side of the

James as I expected. The mine was ordered to be charged, and the morning of the 30th of July was the time fixed for its explosion. I gave Meade minute orders on the 24th directing how I wanted the assault conducted, which orders he amplified into general instructions for the guidance of the troops that were to be engaged.

Meade's instructions, which I, of course, approved most heartily, were all that I can see now was necessary. The only further precaution which he could have taken, and which he could not foresee, would have been to have different men to execute them.

The gallery to the mine was over five hundred feet long from where it entered the ground to the point where it was under the enemy's works, and with a cross gallery of something over eighty feet running under their lines. Eight chambers had been left, requiring a ton of powder each to charge them. All was ready by the time I had prescribed; and on the 29th Hancock and Sheridan were brought back near the James River

with their troops. Under cover of night they started to recross the bridge at Deep Bottom, and to march directly for that part of our lines in front of the mine.

[Gouverneur] Warren was to hold his line of intrenchments with a sufficient number of men and concentrate the balance on the right next to Burnside's corps, while [Edward] Ord, now commanding the 18th corps, temporarily under Meade, was to form in the rear of Burnside to support him when he went in. All were to clear off the

ABOVE: "The Dictator," a huge 13-inch rail-mounted mortar, was one of the most famous siege guns used by the Union at Petersburg.

153

ABOVE: The gabions, trenches, and earthworks used in the construction of the Union's Fort Sedgwick were typical of the passive defenses used by both armies during the siege of Petersburg.

parapets and the *abatis* in their front so as to leave the space as open as possible, and be able to charge the moment the mine had been sprung and Burnside had taken possession. Burnside's corps was not to stop in the crater at all but push on to the top of the hill, supported on the right and left by Ord's and Warren's corps.

Warren and Ord fulfilled their instructions perfectly so far as making ready was concerned. Burnside seemed to have paid no attention whatever to the instructions, and left all the obstruction in his own front for his troops to get over in the best way they could. The four divisions of his corps were commanded by Generals [Robert] Potter, [Orlando] Willcox, [James] Ledlie and [Edward] Ferrero. The last was a colored division; and Burnside selected it to make

the assault. Meade interfered with this. Burnside then took Ledlie's division – a worse selection than the first could have been. In fact, Potter and Willcox were the only division commanders Burnside had who were equal to the occasion. Ledlie besides being otherwise inefficient, proved also to possess disqualification less common among soldiers.

There was some delay about the explosion of the mine so that it did not go off until about five o'clock in the morning. When it did explode it was very successful, making a crater twenty feet deep and something like a hundred feet in length. Instantly one hundred and ten cannon and fifty mortars, which had been placed in the most commanding positions covering the ground to the right and left of where the troops were to enter the enemy's lines, commenced playing. Ledlie's division marched into the crater immediately on the explosion, but most of the men stopped there in the absence of any one to give directions; their commander having found some safe retreat to get into before they started. There was some delay on the left and right in advancing, but some of the troops did get in and turn to the right and left, carrying the rifle-pits as I expected they would do.

There had been great consternation in Petersburg, as we were well aware, about a rumored mine that we were going to explode. They knew we were mining, and they had failed to cut our mine off by countermining, though Beauregard had taken the precaution to run up a line of intrenchments to the rear of that part of their line fronting

ABOVE: Ambrose E. Burnside, commander of the Union's IX Corps, had to bear ultimate responsibility for the great "mine disaster" of July 30.

LEFT: Edward Ferrero led the (black) division originally assigned to exploit the mine explosion, but for political reasons another division was given the task at the last minute – one of the many errors that produced a fiasco.

Wright, saying that a dispatch from Longstreet to Early had been intercepted. It directed the latter to be ready to move and to crush Sheridan as soon as he, Longstreet, arrived. On the receipt of this news Sheridan ordered the cavalry up the valley to join Wright.

On the 18th of October Early was ready to move, and during the night succeeded in getting his troops in the rear of our left flank, which fled precipitately and in great confusion down the valley, losing eighteen pieces of artillery and a thousand or more prisoners. The right under General [George] Getty maintained a firm and steady front, falling back to Middletown where it took a position and made a stand. The cavalry went to the rear, seized the roads leading to Winchester and held them for the use of our troops in falling back, General Wright having ordered a retreat back to that place.

Sheridan having left Washington on the 18th, reached Winchester that night. The following morning he started to join his command. He had scarcely got out of town, when he met his men returning in panic from the front and also heard heavy firing to the south. He immediately ordered the cavalry at Winchester to be deployed across

ABOVE: Like Wickham, James Connor also commanded one of Early's brigades in the Shenandoah. He lost his leg in the fighting there.

LEFT: This Alfred Waud drawing depicts Sheridan's forces as they are pursuing Confederate General Jubal Early's army in the Shenandoah Valley.

the valley to stop the stragglers. Leaving members of his staff to take care of Winchester and the public property there, he set out with a small escort directly for the scene of battle. As he met the fugitives he ordered them to turn back, reminding them that they were going the wrong way. His presence soon restored confidence. Finding themselves worse frightened that hurt the men did halt and turn back. Many of those who had run ten miles got back in time to redeem their reputation as gallant soldiers before night.

When Sheridan got to the front he found Getty and [George Armstrong] Custer still holding their ground firmly between the Confederates and our retreating troops. Everything in the rear was now ordered up.. Sheridan at once proceeded to intrench his position; and he awaited an assault from the enemy. This was made with vigor, and was directed principally against Emory's corps, which had sustained the principal loss in the first attack. By one o'clock the attack was repulsed. Early was so badly damaged that he seemed disinclined to make another attack, but went to work to intrench himself with a view to holding the position he had already gained. He thought, no doubt, that Sheridan would be glad enough to leave him unmolested; but in this he was mistaken.

About the middle of the afternoon Sheridan advanced. He sent his cavalry by both flanks, and they penetrated to the enemy's rear. The contest was close for a time, but at length the left of the enemy broke, and disintegration along the whole line soon followed. Early tried to rally his men, but they were followed so closely that they had to give way very quickly every time they attempted to make a stand. Our cavalry, having pushed on and got in the rear of the Confederates, captured twenty-four pieces of artillery, besides retaking what had been lost in the morning. This victory pretty much closed the campaigning in the Valley of Virginia. All the Confederate troops were sent back to Richmond with the exception of one division of infantry and a little cavalry. Wright's corps was ordered back to the Army of the Potomac, and two other divisions were withdrawn from the valley. Early had lost more men in killed, wounded and captured in the valley than Sheridan had commanded from first to last. . . .

OPPOSITE: William W. Averell (seated) was relieved of his brigade command in Sheridan's Shenandoah army for lack of aggressiveness. Such harsh dealing with subordinates was typical of Sheridan.

BELOW: Alfred Waud's sketch of Sheridan's legendary ride at the Battle of Winchester.

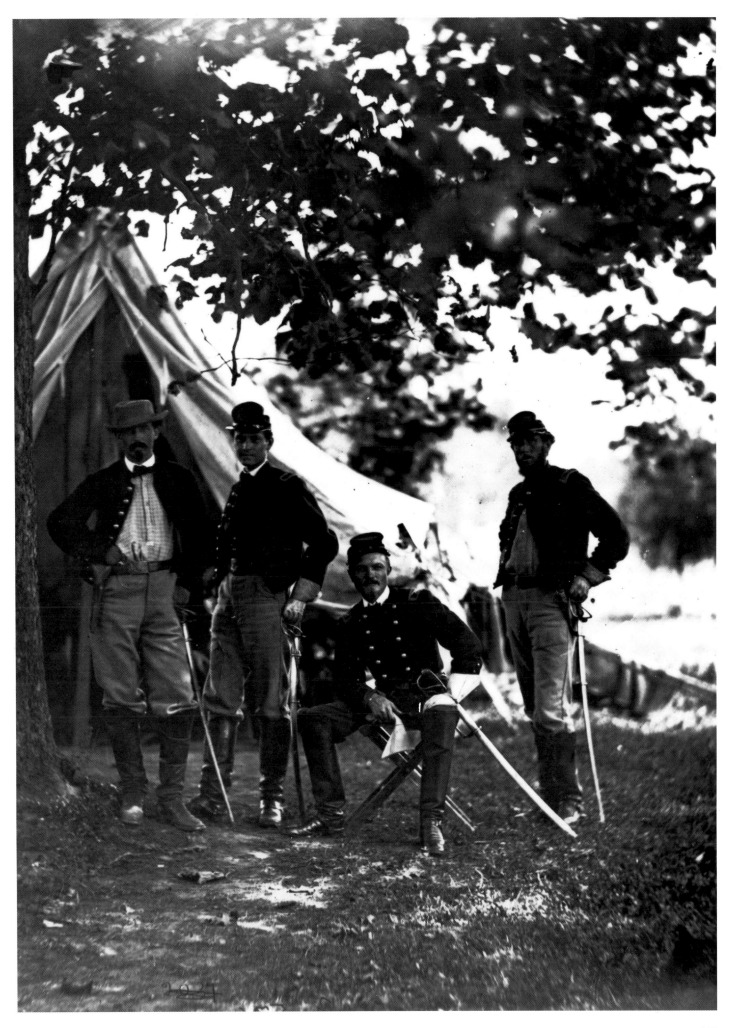

Chapter VII

The Union Victorious

OPPOSITE: Fort McAllister, on the Ogeechee River, was the key to Savannah's outer defenses. Sherman took it on his first try on December 13.

RIGHT: "The Sons of Columbia," a patriotic Union song issued for Independence Day during the war.

BELOW: Sherman's men invade South Carolina, February 1865.

After Sheridan's triumph in the Valley serious campaigning in Virginia halted for the winter, but this was not the case in Georgia. On November 16 Sherman pulled the bulk of his army out of Atlanta and set out on his famous (or, to Southerners, infamous) march through Georgia to Savannah and the sea. The Confederate commander, John B. Hood, had hoped to forestall this move by mounting a diversionary offensive behind Sherman in Tennessee, but Sherman was far too good a strategist to be drawn by such a gambit; instead, he merely detached George Thomas to deal with Hood, while he went on about the more important business of cutting the heart of the South in half.

ABOVE: Sherman's men destroy a Confederate railroad. Even before the March from Atlanta to the Sea it was Sherman's deliberate policy to destroy everything that could be of military value to the enemy.

Thomas proceeded on his assignment with such maddening deliberation that the impatient Grant nearly cashiered him. (As we shall see, later on in his Memoirs *Grant tried to make amends for some of the harsh things he had said about Thomas at the time.) But when Thomas finally did strike Hood, on December 15 in the Battle of Nashville, the effect was devastating: thereafter, for all practical purposes Hood's Army of Tennessee no longer existed.*

Sherman occupied Savannah on December 21, and on February 1, 1865, he embarked on what many historians regard the most brilliant enterprise of his stellar military career, the invasion of the Carolinas. Meanwhile, to the north, Grant was hatching plans for a stroke that he hoped would at last bring the dismal siege of Petersburg to an end. Sheridan, who was essential to the execution of the plan, was temporarily absent, having ridden back into the Shenandoah Valley to mop up what remained of Early's forces, and Grant fretfully awaited his return.

LEFT: The December 15, 1864, Battle of Nashville, in which Union General George Thomas utterly destroyed Hood's Army of Tennessee.

BELOW: Union troops outside Nashville in early December, just before the battle.

169

Sheridan reached City Point on the 26th day of March. His horses, of course, were jaded and many of them had lost their shoes. A few days of rest were necessary to recuperate the animals and also to have them shod and put in condition for moving. Immediately on General Sheridan's arrival at City Point I prepared his instructions for the move which I had decided upon. The movement was to commence on the 29th of the month.

After reading the instructions I had given him, Sheridan walked out of my tent, and I followed to have some conversation with him by himself – not in the presence of anybody else, even of a member of my staff. In preparing his instructions I contemplated just what took place; that is to say, capturing Five Forks, driving the enemy from Petersburg and Richmond and terminating the contest before separating from the enemy. But the Nation had already become restless and discouraged at the prolongation of the war, and many believed that it would never terminate except by compromise. Knowing that unless my plan proved an entire success it would be interpreted as a disastrous defeat, I provided in these instructions that in a certain event he was to cut loose from the Army of the Potomac and his base of supplies, and living upon the country proceed south by the way of the Danville Rail-

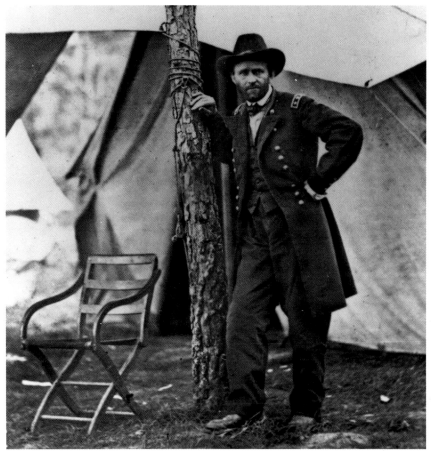

ABOVE: Santa Claus
Sherman gives the North
a Christmas present in a
*Frank Leslie's Illustrated
Newspaper* cartoon.

BELOW: Savannah in 1864.

RIGHT: The burden of
command is all too
evident in this famous
informal portrait of an
exhausted and careworn
Grant at the height of the
1864 campaign.

OPPOSITE: Grant's plan for ending the Petersburg siege in the spring of 1865 was almost wholly dependent on whether Sheridan could turn Lee's flank. "Little Phil" would not let Grant down.

LEFT: Mantled Union guns before Petersburg.

BELOW: "Bomb-proof" quarters at Union Fort Sedgwick (a.k.a. "Fort Hell") in 1865.

road, or near it, across the Roanoke, get in the rear of Johnston, who was guarding that road, and co-operate with Sherman in destroying Johnston; then with these combined forces to help carry out the instructions which Sherman already had received, to act in co-operation with the armies around Petersburg and Richmond.

I saw that after Sheridan had read his instructions he seemed somewhat disappointed at the idea, possibly, of having to cut loose again from the Army of the Potomac, and place himself between the two main armies of the enemy. I said to him: "General, this portion of your instructions I have put in merely as a blind;" and gave him the reason for doing so. . . . I told him that, as a matter of fact, I intended to close the war right here, with this movement, and that he should go no farther. His face at once brightened up, and slapping his hand on his leg he said: "I am glad to hear it, and we can do it." . . .

Finally the 29th of March came, and fortunately there having been a few days free from rain, the surface of the ground was dry, giving indications that the time had come when we could move. On that date I moved out with all the army available after leaving sufficient force to hold the line about Petersburg. . . . The next day, March 30th, we had made sufficient progress to the south-west to warrant me in starting Sheridan with his cavalry over by Dinwiddie with instructions to then come up by the road leading northwest to Five Forks, thus menacing the right of Lee's line. . . .

My hope was that Sheridan would be able to carry Five Forks, get on the enemy's right flank and rear, and force them to weaken their centre to protect their right so that an assault in the centre might be successfully made. General Wright's corps had been designated to make this assault, which I intended to order as soon as information reached me of Sheridan's success. He was to move under cover as close to the enemy as he could get. . . .

Sheridan succeeded by the middle of the afternoon [of April 1st] or a little later, in advancing up to the point from which to make his designed assault upon Five Forks itself. He was very impatient to make the assault and have it all over before night, because the ground he occupied would be untenable for him in bivouac during the night. Unless the assault was made and was successful, he would be obliged to return to Dinwiddie Court-House, or even further than that for the night. . . .

It was dusk when our troops under Sheri-

BELOW: Sheridan approaches Five Forks on April 1, 1965. The battle that ensued would mark the beginning of the end of the Civil War.

dan went over the parapets of the enemy. The two armies were mingled together there for a time in such manner that it was almost a question which one was going to demand the surrender of the other. Soon, however, the enemy broke and ran in every direction; some six thousand prisoners, beside artillery and small-arms in large quantities, falling into our hands. The flying troops were pursued in different directions, the cavalry and 5th corps under Sheridan pursuing the larger body which moved north-west.

This pursuit continued until about nine o'clock at night, when Sheridan halted his troops, and knowing the importance to him of the part of the enemy's line which had been captured, returned, sending the 5th corps across Hatcher's Run to just southwest of Petersburg, and facing them toward it. [Wesley] Merritt, with the cavalry, stopped and bivouacked west of Five Forks.

This was the condition which affairs were in on the night of the 1st of April. I then issued orders for an assault by Wright and

[John] Parke at four o'clock on the morning of the 2d. I also ordered the 2d corps, General [Andrew] Humphreys, and General Ord with the Army of the James, on the left, to hold themselves in readiness to take any advantage that could be taken from weakening in their front. . . .

I was afraid that Lee would regard the possession of Five Forks as of so much importance that he would make a last desperate effort to retake it, risking everything upon the cast of a single die. It was for this reason that I had ordered the assault to take place at once, as soon as I had received the news of the capture of Five Forks. The corps commanders, however, reported that it was so dark that the men could not see to move, and it would be impossible to make the assault then. But we kept up a continuous artillery fire upon the enemy around the whole line including that north of the James River, until it was light enough to move, which was about a quarter to five in the morning.

BELOW: Victorious Federals pursue fleeing Rebel troops at Five Forks on April 1.

them, and at last accounts was engaged with them. Not knowing whether Sheridan would get up in time, General Humphreys was sent with another division from here. The whole captures since the army started out gunning will amount to not less than twelve thousand men, and probably fifty pieces of artillery. I do not know the number of men and guns accurately. . . .

I think the President might come out and pay us a visit tomorrow.

U. S. GRANT,
Lieutenant-General.

During the night of April 2d our line was intrenched from the river above to the river below. I ordered a bombardment to be commenced the next morning at five A.M., to be followed by an assault at six o'clock; but the enemy evacuated Petersburg early in the morning. . . .

The fall of Petersburg doomed Richmond, which was occupied by Union troops the following day. Lee's army, now down to about 35,000 starving men and beginning to disintegrate, fled westward toward Amelia Court House, where Lee hoped to entrain his troops on the Danville Railroad and take them to South Carolina to join forces with Joseph Johnston in his fight against Sherman. But Sheridan cut the Danville line on April 5, and Lee's last hope of escape was gone. What was left of the Army of Northern Virginia struggled on for a few more days, but on April 9, at Appomattox Court House, Lee was finally brought to bay and surrounded by overwhelmingly superior Union forces. It was the end. "There is nothing left for me to do but go and see General Grant," said Lee, "and I would rather die a thousand deaths." A few moments later a Southern rider bearing a white flag galloped towards the Union lines.

BELOW: Union cavalry horses stand tethered to an iron fence amid Richmond's ruins.

When the white flag was put out by Lee, as already described, I was [en route] moving towards Appomattox Court House, and consequently could not be communicated with immediately, and be informed of what Lee had done. Lee, therefore, sent a flag to the rear to advise Meade and one to the front to Sheridan, saying that he had sent a message to me for the purpose of having a meeting to consult about the surrender of his army, and asked for a suspension of hostilities until I could be communicated with. As they had heard nothing of this until the fighting had got to be severe and all going against Lee, both of these commanders hesitated very considerably about suspending hostilities at all. They were afraid it was not in good faith, and we had the Army of Northern Virginia where it could not escape except by some deception. They, however, finally consented to a suspension of hostilities for two hours to give an opportunity of communicating with me in that time, if possible. It was found that, from the route I had taken, they would probably not be able to communicate with me and get an answer back within the time fixed unless the messenger should pass through the rebel lines.

Lee, therefore, sent an escort with the officer bearing this message through his lines to me.

April 9, 1865

GENERAL:– I received your note of this morning on the picket-line whither I had come to meet you and ascertain definitely what terms were embraced in your proposal of yesterday, with reference to the surrender of this army. I now request an interview in accordance with the offer contained in your letter of yesterday for that purpose.

R. E. LEE, General
LIEUTENANT-GENERAL U. S. GRANT

When the officer reached me I was still suffering with [a] sick headache; but the instant I saw the contents of the note I was cured. I wrote the following note in reply and hastened on:

April 9, 1865.

GENERAL R. E. LEE,

Commanding C. S. Armies

Your note of this date is but this moment (11.50 A.M.) received, in consequence of my having passed from the Richmond and Lynchburg road to the Farmville and Lynchburg road. I am at this writing about four miles west of Walker's Church and will push forward to the front for the purpose of meeting you. Notice sent to me on this road where you wish the interview to take place will meet me.

U. S. GRANT,
Lieutenant-General.

I was conducted at once to where Sheridan was located with his troops drawn up in line of battle facing the Confederate army near by. They were very much excited, and expressed their view that this was all a ruse employed to enable the Confederates to get away. They said they believed that Johnston was marching up from North Carolina now, and Lee was moving to join him; and they would whip the rebels where they now were in five minutes if I would only let them go in. But I had no doubt about the good faith of Lee, and pretty soon was conducted to where he was. I found him at the house of a Mr. McLean, at Appomattox Court House, with Colonel Marshall, one of his staff officers, awaiting my arrival. The head of his column was occupying a hill, on a portion of which was an apple orchard, beyond a little valley which separated it from that on the crest of which Sheridan's forces were drawn up in line of battle to the south. . . .

OPPOSITE TOP: The last C.S.A. general in Richmond, Martin W. Gary, escorted Jefferson Davis to (temporary) safety in South Carolina.

OPPOSITE BOTTOM: Not all the Rebel troops in Richmond fled the city. Some, as shown in this Waud sketch, took the city's fall as an occasion to surrender.

BELOW: The house of Wilmer McLean in Appomattox Court House, Virginia. McLean's former house had been ruined in the Civil War's first big battle, First Bull Run. In this house the war would effectively end.

I had known General Lee in the old army, and had served with him in the Mexican War; but did not suppose, owing to the difference in our age and rank, that he would remember me; while I would more naturally remember him distinctly, because he was the chief of staff of General Scott in the Mexican War.

When I had left camp that morning I had not expected so soon the result that was then taking place, and consequently was in rough garb. I was without a sword, as I usually was when on horseback on the field, and wore a soldier's blouse for a coat, with

BELOW: Union General Orville Babcock (right) was Grant's aide-de-camp. It was he who was sent to escort General Lee to the surrender talks at the McLean house.

the shoulder straps of my rank to indicate to the army who I was. When I went into the house I found General Lee. We greeted each other, and after shaking hands took our seats. I had my staff with me, a good portion of whom were in the room during the whole of the interview.

What General Lee's feelings were I do not know. As he was a man of much dignity, with an impassible face, it was impossible to say whether he felt inwardly glad that the end had finally come, or felt sad over the result, and was too manly to show it. Whatever his feelings, they were entirely concealed from my observation; but my own feelings, which had been quite jubilant on the receipt of his letter, were sad and depressed. I felt like anything rather than rejoicing at the downfall of a foe who had fought so long and valiantly, and had suffered so much for a cause, though that cause was, I believe, one of the worst for which a people ever fought, and one for which there was the least excuse. I do not question, however, the sincerity of the great mass of those who were opposed to us.

General Lee was dressed in a full uniform which was entirely new, and was wearing a sword of considerable value, very likely the sword which had been presented by the State of Virginia; at all events, it was an entirely different sword from the one that would ordinarily be worn in the field. In my rough traveling suit, the uniform of a private with the straps of a lieutenant-general, I must have contrasted very strangely with a man so handsomely dressed, six feet high and of faultless form. But this was not a matter that I thought of until afterwards.

We soon fell into a conversation about old army times. He remarked that he remembered me very well in the old army; and I told him that as a matter of course I remembered him perfectly, but from the difference in our rank and years (there being about sixteen

years' difference in our ages), I had thought it very likely that I had not attracted his attention sufficiently to be remembered by him after such a long interval. Our conversation grew so pleasant that I almost forgot the object of our meeting. After the conversation had run on in this style for some time, General Lee called my attention to the object of our meeting, and said that he had asked for this interview for the purpose of getting from me the terms I proposed to give his

ABOVE: General Robert Edward Lee, the greatest commander of the Confederacy.

LEFT: A portion of a note from Lee to Grant, part of the historic correspondence between the two commanders regarding Lee's surrender.

THE SURRENDER OF GEN. LEE AND HIS ARMY TO LIEUT. GEN. GRANT

HONOR THE ILLUSTRIOUS DEAD, AND HEARTILY SYMPATHIZE WITH THE SUFFERINGS OF OUR GALLANT HEROES AND THEIR FAMILIES.

army. I said that I meant merely that his army should lay down their arms, not to take them up again during the continuance of the war unless duly and properly exchanged. He said that he had so understood my letter.

Then we gradually fell off again into conversation about matters foreign to the subject which had brought us together. This continued for some little time, when General Lee again interrupted the course of the conversation by suggesting that the terms I proposed to give his army ought to be written out. I called to General [Ely] Parker, secretary on my staff, for writing materials, and commenced writing out the following terms:

APPOMATTOX C. H., Va.,
Apl 9th, 1865.
GEN. R. E. LEE,
Comd'g C. S. A.

GEN: In accordance with the substance of my letter to you of the 8th inst., I propose to receive the surrender of the Army of N. Va. on the following terms, to wit: Rolls of all the officers and men to be made in duplicate. One copy to be given to an officer designated by me, the other to be retained by such officer or officers as you may designate. The officers to give their individual paroles not to take up arms against

the Government of the United States until properly exchanged, and each company or regimental commander sign a like parole for the men of their commands. The arms, artillery and public property to be parked and stacked, and turned over to the officer appointed by me to receive them. This will not embrace the side-arms of the officers, nor their private horses or baggage. This done, each officer and man will be allowed to return to their homes, not to be disturbed by United States authority so long as they observe their paroles and the laws in force where they may reside.

Very respectfully,
U. S. GRANT,
Lt. Gen.

When I put my pen to the paper I did not know the first word that I should make use of in writing the terms. I only knew what was in my mind, and I wished to express it clearly, so that there could be no mistaking it. As I wrote on, the thought occurred to me that the officers had their own private horses and effects, which were important to them, but of no value to us; also that it would be an unnecessary humiliation to call upon them to deliver their side arms.

No conversation, not one word, passed between General Lee and myself, either

ABOVE: The April 9 meeting between Lee and Grant in the McLean house, where the terms upon which Lee surrendered were formally concluded.

OPPOSITE: None of the many artists' versions of Lee's surrender to Grant is fully authentic or even terribly convincing. This one is the work of *Harper's Weekly's* famous Thomas Nast.

RIGHT AND OPPOSITE: Victor and vanquished – Grant and Lee as they looked in 1865. Arguments about who was the better general probably can never be resolved. Both men accomplished things the other did not. Grant never won a battle as dazzling as Lee's famous victory at Chancellorsville; Lee never fought a campaign as brilliant as the one Grant waged against Vicksburg. It is enough to say that both were truly great commanders.

OPPOSITE: One of the most beloved of American icons: Mathew Brady's famed January 8, 1864, portrait of Abraham Lincoln.

BELOW: Lincoln's cabinet in 1863. In the foreground, facing Lincoln, is Secretary of State William Seward, who was badly wounded by Lewis Paine in the execution of the Booth assassination plot.

characteristics of the President. With Mr. Stanton the case is different. They were the very opposite of each other in almost every particular, except that each possessed great ability. Mr. Lincoln gained influence over men by making them feel that it was a pleasure to serve him. He preferred yielding his own wish to gratify others, rather than to insist upon having his own way. It distressed him to disappoint others. In matters of public duty, however, he had what he wished, but in the least offensive way. Mr. Stanton never questioned his own authority to command, unless resisted. He cared nothing for the feeling of others. In fact it seemed to be pleasanter to him to disappoint than to gratify. He felt no hesitation in assuming the functions of the executive, or in acting without advising with him. If his act was not sustained, he would change it – if he saw the matter would be followed up until he did so.

It was generally supposed that these two officials formed the complement of each other. The Secretary was required to prevent the President's being imposed upon. The President was required in the more responsible place of seeing that injustice was not done to others. I do not know that this view of these two men is still entertained by the majority of the people. It is not a correct view, however, in my estimation. Mr. Lincoln did not require a guardian to aid him in the fulfilment of a public trust.

Mr. Lincoln was not timid, and he was willing to trust his generals in making and executing their plans. The Secretary was very timid, and it was impossible for him to avoid interfering with the armies covering the capital when it was sought to defend it by an offensive movement against the army guarding the Confederate capital. He could see our weakness, but he could not see that the enemy was in danger. The enemy would not have been in danger if Mr. Stanton had been in the field. These characteristics of the two officials were clearly shown shortly after Early came so near getting into the capital.

Among the army and corps commanders who served with me during the war between the States, and who attracted much public attention, but of whose ability as soldiers I have not yet given any estimate, are Meade, Hancock, Sedgwick, Burnside, Terry and Hooker. . . . Of those first named, Burnside at one time had command of the Army of the

RIGHT: Union General Ambrose Burnside receives command of the Army of the Potomac in 1862. Burnside had insisted that he was not up to the post, and soon Washington wished it had listened to him.

BELOW: The Union victory at the Battle of the Gettysburg in 1863 made the reputation of George Meade, who took the command of the Army of the Potomac on June 28, three days before the battle.

Potomac, and later of the Army of the Ohio. Hooker also commanded the Army of the Potomac for a short time.

General [George] Meade was an officer of great merit, with drawbacks to his usefulness that were beyond his control. He had been an officer of the engineer corps before the war, and consequently had never served with troops until he was over forty-six years of age. He never had, I believe, a command of less than a brigade. He saw clearly and distinctly the position of the enemy, and the topography of the country in front of his own position. His first idea was to take advantage of the lay of the ground, sometimes without reference to the direction we wanted to move afterwards. He was subordinate to his superiors in rank to the extent that he could execute an order which changed his own plans with the same zeal he would have displayed if the plan had been his own. He was brave and conscientious, and commanded the respect of all who knew him. He was unfortunately of a temper that would get beyond his control, at times, and make him speak to officers of high rank in the most offensive manner. No one saw this fault more plainly than he himself, and no one regretted it more. This made it unpleasant at times, even in battle, for those around him to approach him even with information. In spite of this defect he was a most valuable officer and deserves a high place in the annals of his country.

General [Ambrose] Burnside was an officer who was generally liked and respected. He was not, however, fitted to command an army. No one knew this better than himself. He always admitted his blunders, and extenuated those of officers under him beyond what they were entitled to. It was hardly his fault that he was ever assigned to a separate command.

Of [Joseph] Hooker I saw but little during the war. I had known him very well before, however. Where I did see him, at Chattanooga, his achievement in bringing his command around the point of Lookout Mountain

BELOW: Meade with his staff in 1863. Regarding Meade's notoriously bad temper, one member of his staff wrote, "I don't know any thin old gentleman . . . who, when he is wrathy, exercises less of Christian charity than my well-beloved chief."

Robert E. Lee

Chapter I

The Seven Days' Campaign

In the winter of 1862 the Confederate Congress created the office of "military adviser to the President," with the view of lightening the arduous duties which devolved upon him as commander-in-chief of the Confederate forces. Lee was selected to fill this position, and about the 13th of March, 1862, he entered upon his duties. The staff allowed him consisted of a military secretary with the rank of colonel and four aides with the rank of major. General Lee offered to Major A. L. Long the position of military secretary, and selected for his aides-de-camp Majors Randolph Talcott, Walter H. Taylor, Charles S. Venable, and Charles Marshall. When the writer reported for duty, about the middle of May, he found the general actively engaged in superintending the erection of defences on the James River near Richmond. The battery and obstruc-

tions at Drewry's Bluff were so advanced that the great alarm that had been felt for the safety of the city upon the evacuation of Norfolk began to subside, as there was no longer the fear of an immediate attack. The Federal gunboats had entered the James, and on the 15th the battery at Drewry's Bluff was attacked by the enemy's fleet, consisting of the iron-clads Galena and Naugatuck, a monitor, and two gunboats. These vessels were skilfully handled and gallantly fought. The Galena approached within four hundred yards of the battery, and then opened a spirited fire with her powerful guns; the Naugatuck and monitor closely supported her, while the gunboats delivered their fire at a longer range. After a hotly-contested conflict the fleet was repulsed with heavy loss. The Galena was so severely damaged as to be rendered unfit for future

RIGHT: Confederate General Joseph E. Johnston was wounded at the Battle of Seven Pines. President Davis named Lee to replace him as commander of the Army of Northern Virginia.

BELOW: Confederate soldiers wounded in the Battle of Seven Pines are attended by civilians in the streets of Richmond.

service, while the other vessels were more or less injured; the battery sustained but slight damage. This defeat of the gunboats by an incomplete earthwork of only five guns for the first time caused a just value to be placed on defences of that character, which thenceforth became a conspicuous element in defensive operations.

At this time the safety of Richmond was entirely due to the skill and energy of General Lee, for upon the evacuation of Norfolk the James was left enirely open from its mouth to Richmond, and the hastily-constructed defence at Drewry's Bluff was the only barrier interposed between that city and a hostile fleet. After crossing the Chickahominy, about the 20th, General J. E. Johnston assumed the defence of Richmond. He attacked the enemy at Seven Pines on the 31st of May, and was severely wounded, as we have seen, near the close of the action. That event was immediately followed by the appointment of Lee to the command of the Army of Northern Virginia. Though regretting the cause that led to his assignment to the command of the army, he was pleased to be released from the duties of the office for those of the field, which were far better suited to his active and energetic disposition. He carried with him to the field the same personal staff that had been allowed him in Richmond.

On the afternoon of the 1st of June, General G. W. Smith, on whom the command of the army had devolved when General Johnston was wounded, resigned his command to General Lee, and shortly after retired on account of bad health. It soon appeared that there was considerable depression in the army, the natural consequence of the incidents of war. As some of the officers were apprehensive that the army would not be able to maintain its position should it be attacked, Lee thought it advisable to assemble his principal officers for deliberation on its condition at an early period.

In reference to this point, Mr. Davis, in his *Rise and Fall of the Confederacy*, chap. xxiii., vol. ii., says: "The day after General Lee assumed command I was riding out to the army, when I saw at a house on my left a number of horses, and among them one I recognized as belonging to him. I dismounted and entered the house, where I found him in consultation with a number of his general officers. The tone of the conversation was quite despondent, and one especially pointed out the inevitable consequence of the enemy's advance by throwing out bayoux and constructing successive parallels." Farther on he refers to a want of co-operation that existed among the different divisions during the battle of Fair Oaks and Seven Pines, which was productive of natural distrust that might have resulted in serious demoralization had it not been

ABOVE: Federal reconnaissance balloon *Intrepid* at the Battle of Seven Pines on June 1, 1862.

ABOVE: As the Confederates moved to defend Richmond, they were engaged by Federal troops at Williamsburg on the James.

RIGHT: Union charge at Seven Pines. The Confederate defense, in which General Johnston was wounded, caused the Federals to withdraw temporarily, although they continued to threaten the Southern capital.

speedily corrected. The council met, as had been previously ordered, on the Nine Mile road, near the house which had been occupied by Smith as his headquarters.

The principal officers of the army were present, and were almost unanimous in the opinion that the line then occupied should be abandoned for one nearer Richmond which was considered more defensible.

The line in question was that which had been adopted by Johnston prior to the occupation in force of the south bank of the Chickahominy by the enemy, and was the strongest the country presented; but now the dispirited condition of our troops and the occupation in force by the enemy of the south side of the river caused the most prominent Confederate officers to doubt their ability to hold it, and consequently they urged its evacuation and withdrawal to a position nearer Richmond. Lee thus found himself in a situation of great embarrassment. He did not then possess the fame he was destined soon to acquire. He was also unknown to that army, and lacked its confidence. Under these disadvantages he was obliged to assume the responsibility of maintaining a position pronounced untenable by his principal officers, or of hazarding the safety of Richmond by a withdrawal of his forces that would inevitably result in a forced occupation of the outer defences of the capital and its complete investiture by the enemy, which would have ensured the speedy capture of the city. Lee, who had long been accustomed to rely upon himself, quickly decided on the course to be adopted. It was evident that the present position of the army must be maintained or that Richmond must be abandoned to the enemy, and the loss of Richmond at this time would have been of incalculable injury to the Confederate cause. He therefore, in opposition to the opinion of his subordinates, determined to hold the position in which he found the army; but before making known his determination he made a careful reconnoissance of the whole position, and then declared his intention of holding it, ordering it to be immediately fortified in the most effective manner.

General Lee then reorganized his forces and established a strong defensive line. He selected, with slight alterations, the position then occupied by his troops. This line extended from Chaffin's Bluff, on the James River, crossing the river road about four miles, and the Darby Town, Charles City,

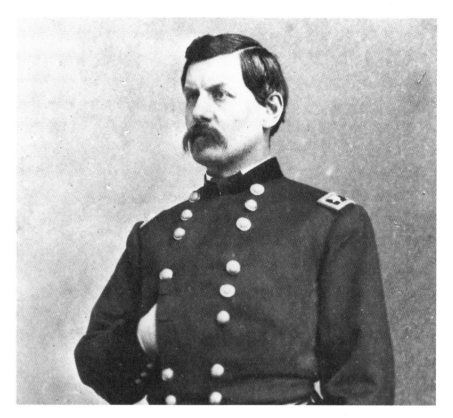

Williamsburg, and Nine Mile roads, about five miles from Richmond to a point on the Chickahominy a little above New Bridge, and then continued up that stream to Meadow Bridge. The army consisted of six divisions. Longstreet's division formed the right, while those of Huger, D. H. Hill, Magruder, Whiting, and A. P. Hill, in the order named, extended to the left. The division of A. P. Hill constituted the left of the Confederate position. The greater part of Stuart's cavalry was on the left, picketing on the Rappahannock and having a small force in observation at Fredericksburg. The duty of constructing a fortified line was apportioned among the divisions, each commander being responsible for the defence in his own front. Very soon a continuous line of breastworks appeared, and as these arose the spirits of the men revived and the sullen silence with which their labor began gave place to jokes and laughter. Those who had entered upon the work with reluctance now felt recompensed by the sense of safety it gave them. The defences daily increased until they were sufficiently strong to resist any attack that was likely to be made upon them. In the mean time the stragglers and convalescents began to return, and the army gradually increased. Lee daily appeared upon the lines, and after a few days his presence inspired the troops with confidence and enthusiasm. McClellan established his headquarters on the south side of the

ABOVE: Union General James B. McClellan's Army of the Potomac faced six entrenched divisions of Lee's Army of Northern Virginia as it crossed the Chickahominy in its advance toward Richmond.

223

Chickahominy about the same time that Lee assumed the command of the Army of Northern Virginia. The Federal army, after deducting the casualties of the late battle, amounted to about 100,000 men for duty; 75,000 of this force were on the south side of the Chickahominy, the remainder on the north of that stream, extending as high up as Mechanicsville. From this position a junction would be easily formed with McDowell's corps of 40,000 men, which, although a part of McClellan's forces, was persistently held in the neighborhood of Fredericksburg as a covering force for Washington.

*   *   *

Lee's headquarters at this time were on the Nine Mile road, a position which gave him a good oversight of the army and brought all portions of the lines within easy reach. Yet the batteries, rifle-pits, and earthworks which had been erected with so much labor under his personal supervision were destined to have no further utility than that already adverted to – the infusion of confidence into the previously dispirited army. It was not the purpose of the commanding general to remain upon the defensive and await the slow but sure advances of the enemy. He, on the contrary, formed the bolder decision of hurling the force under his command against the serried battalions of the foe, as indicated in the last-quoted extract from the notebook (*Deleted – Ed.*).

When McClellan crossed the Chickahominy it was thought he would advance immediately upon Richmond. This expectation was disappointed, however, for instead of advancing he began to fortify his position. The right wing rested on the Chickahominy a little below New Bridge, and the left extended to the White Oak Swamp, embracing a front of about four miles, nearly parallel with that of the Confederates. The opposing lines were separated by an interval but little exceeding a mile, but each was obscured from the other's view by the intervening forest. The picket-lines were often within close musket-range of each other. At first there was a good deal of picket-skirmishing, but this was soon discontinued by mutual consent, and a lively exchange of newspapers, coffee, and tobacco succeeded it. The strength of the Confederate force was always greatly over-estimated by McClellan, and his frequent and urgent calls for re-

BELOW: In an engraving made from a field sketch, Federal pickets are shown defending against a Confederate attack as reinforcements arrive.

column had passed a few days previously.

Thoroughfare Gap was reached about noon of the 28th. It was quickly found to be occupied by a Federal force. Some slight attempt was made to dislodge the enemy, but without success, as their position proved too strong, and it seemed as if the movement of the Confederate army in that direction was destined to be seriously interfered with. Meanwhile, nothing further had been heard from Jackson, and there was a natural anxiety in regard to his position and possible peril. Unless the mountains could speedily be passed by Longstreet's corps the force under Jackson might be assailed by the whole of Pope's army, and very severely dealt with.

Under these critical circumstances General Lee made every effort to find some available route over the mountains, sending reconnoissances to right and left in search of a practicable pass. Some of the officers ascended the mountain during the evening, and perceived from its summit a large force which lay in front of the Gap. Meanwhile, the sound of cannonading was audible from the other side of the range, and it was evident that an engagement was taking place.

* * *

Fortunately, circumstances favored the Confederate cause. One of the reconnoitering parties found a woodchopper, who told them of an old road over the mountain to which he could guide them, and which might be practicable for infantry. Hood was at once directed to make an effort to lead his division across the mountain by this route. This he succeeded in doing, and the head of his column reached the other side of the range by morning. Another route had also been discovered by which Wilcox was enabled to turn the Gap.

In the mean time, Pope himself had been playing into the hands of his adversary. He had ordered McDowell to retire from the Gap and join him to aid in the anticipated crushing of Jackson. McDowell did so, leaving Rickett's division to hold the Gap. In evident ignorance of the vicinity of Longstreet's corps, this force was also withdrawn during the night, and on the morning of the 29th Lee found the Gap unoccupied, and at once marched through at the head of Longstreet's column. On reaching Gainesville, three miles beyond the Gap, he found Stuart, who informed him of Jackson's situation. The division was at once marched into position

on Jackson's right.

Pope had unknowingly favored the advance of the Confederate commander. His removal of McDowell from his position had been a tactical error of such magnitude that it could not well be retrieved. The object of the movement had been to surround Jackson at Manassas Junction, upon which place the several corps of the army were marching by various routes. Pope wrote in his order to McDowell, "If you will march promptly and rapidly at the earliest dawn upon Manassas Junction, we shall bag the whole crowd." The scheme was a good one, but for two unconsidered contingencies. Had Jackson awaited the enemy at Manassas Junction, he would have found himself in a trap. But he did not choose to do so. When the van of the Federal columns reached the Junction, they found that the bird had flown. And Longstreet's corps,

ABOVE: In an engraving from a field drawing by A. R. Waud, General Robert E. Lee is seen observing the skirmishing at Thoroughfare Gap.

BELOW: General McDowell's camp at Manassas. The Union force arrived too late at Manassas Junction to trap the forewarned General Jackson.

MAP Nº 3.
OPERATIONS
OF THE
ARMY OF VIRGINIA
under Maj. Gen. JOHN POPE
POSITION OF TROOPS
ON THE NIGHT OF
August 27th 1862

W. Hoelcke, Capt. and Add'l Aide-de-Camp U.S.A.

United States Forces
Rebels

Scale of Miles

To accompany report of Maj Gen. John Pope, U S Army.
SERIES 1. VOL XII. PART 2. PAGE 12.

ABOVE: Map accompanying Pope's report on the battles records the positions of troops on both sides on the night of August 27.

OPPOSITE TOP: Map showing the action of August 28.

OPPOSITE BOTTOM: A Currier & Ives print attempts to show the ferocity of the fighting at Bull Run on August 29.

which might have been prevented from passing the Bull Run range, had been given free opportunity to cross to the aid of Jackson, who on the night of the 27th and morning of the 28th left the Junction and made a rapid march to the westward. The error was a fatal one to the hopes of the boasting Western general.

The cannonade at the Gap on the 28th had informed Jackson of Lee's proximity. He at once took a position north of the Warrenton turnpike, his left resting on Bull Run, near Sudley Church, and his right extending toward Gainesville. The distance of this position from the Warrenton road varied from one to two miles, the greater part of the left embracing a railroad cut, while the centre and right occupied a commanding ridge. In this position Jackson could easily unite with Lee on his passing Thoroughfare Gap, or, failing in that and being hard pressed, he could retire by the east end of Bull Run Mountain and unite with Lee on the north side of that mountain. The divisions of Ewell and Taliaferro formed the right and

centre of Jackson's line of battle, while that of A. P. Hill constituted his left. Jackson had barely completed his arrangements when a heavy column of Federal infantry (King's division of McDowell's corps) appeared on the Warrenton turnpike. In order to delay its advance several batteries were placed in position, which by a well-directed fire caused them to halt; at the same time Jackson ordered Taliaferro to deploy one brigade across the Warrenton turnpike, holding his other brigades in reserve. Ewell was directed to support him. About three o'clock the Federals bore down in heavy force upon Ewell and Taliaferro, who maintained their positions with admirable firmness, repelling attack after attack until night. The loss on both sides was considerable. Among the wounded on the side of the Confederates were Generals Taliaferro and Ewell, the latter seriously, having to lose his leg.

Jackson, with barely 20,000 men, now found himself confronted by the greater part of the Federal army. Any commander with less firmness would have sought safety in

MAP Nº 4.

OPERATIONS
OF THE
ARMY OF VIRGINIA
under Maj. Gen. JOHN POPE

POSITION OF TROOPS
AT SUNSET
August 28th 1862.

W. Hoelcke, Capt. and Add'l Aide-de-Camp U.S.A.

—— United States Forces
—— Rebels
⊠ Old Rebel works

Scale : Half an Inch to the Mile

To accompany report of Maj. Gen. John Pope. U.S. Army
SERIES 1 VOL. XII. PART 2 PAGE 12.

ABOVE: Ruins of Stone Bridge on the blasted battlefield at Bull Run.

retreat. But having heard the Confederate guns at Thoroughfare Gap, he knew that Lee would join him the next day. Therefore he determined to hold his position at all hazards.

By the morning of the 29th, as we have already described, Hood's division had reached the south side of the mountain, and early in the day was joined by the remainder of Longstreet's corps by way of the open Gap.

While these important movements were in progress, Pope had resumed his attack upon Jackson, and was pressing him with his whole force, hoping to crush him before he could be relieved by Lee. On the arrival of Lee, Pope discontinued his attack, and retired to the position which the year before had been the scene of the famous battle of Bull Run, or Manassas. Lee then took a position opposite, with Longstreet's corps occupying a lower range of hills extending across and at right angles to the Warrenton turn-

pike, while Jackson occupied the line of railroad before mentioned, which, slightly deviating from the general direction of Longstreet's position, formed with it an obtuse crotchet, opening toward the enemy. An elevated ridge connecting Jackson's right with Longstreet's left, forming the centre of the Confederate position, was strongly occupied with artillery to fill the interval between Longstreet and Jackson. The hills on the right, were crowned by the Washington Artillery, commanded by Colonel Walton. The remainder of the artillery was distributed at prominent points throughout the line, while Stuart's cavalry covered its flanks and observed the movements of the enemy. Since Pope's retreat from Culpeper Courthouse he had been frequently reinforced by detachments from the armies of McClellan and Burnside. The greater part of those armies having now joined him, and the remainder being in supporting-distance, his arrogance revived, and, being sure of an easy victory, he sent the most sanguine despatches to the authorities at Washington. In preparation for battle he took a position embracing a succession of low ridges, nearly parallel to, and about a mile from, the line assumed by Lee. About midway between the two armies lay a narrow valley, through which meandered a small brook, whose low murmurs seemed to invite the weary soldier to slake his thirst with its cool and limpid waters. The afternoon of the 29th was principally occupied in preparation. Longstreet's corps, on the right, was formed in two lines. Jackson, on the left, having been considerably reduced by rapid marching and hard fighting, could present only a single line with a small reserve.

On the morning of the 30th an ominous silence pervaded both armies. Each seemed to be taking the measure of its antagonist.

Lee saw threatening him the armies of Pope, McClellan, and Burnside, whose combined strength exceeded 150,000 men, while his own army was less than 60,000 strong. Notwithstanding this disparity of numbers, the presence of Lee, Jackson, and Longstreet inspired the troops with confidence far exceeding their numerical strength. About eight o'clock the Federal batteries opened a lively cannonade upon the Confederate centre, which was responded to with spirit by the battalions of Colonel Stephen D. Lee and Major Shoemaker. This practice having continued for an hour, both sides relapsed into silence. This was the prelude to the approaching contest. Between twelve and one o'clock the cannonade was resumed in earnest. The thunder of cannon shook the hills, while shot and shell, shrieking and hissing, filled the air, and the sulphurous

BELOW: Men of Company C, 41st New York Infantry at Manassas before the start of the battles. In a month, a total of 25,000 Union and Confederate soldiers who took part in the Second Bull Run campaign would be dead, wounded or missing.

smoke, settling in black clouds along the intervening valley, hung like a pall over the heavy columns of infantry which rushed into the "jaws of death." Pope, having directed his principal attack upon the Confederate left, advanced his infantry in powerful force against Jackson, whose single line behind the friendly shelter of railroad cuts and embankments received this mighty array with tremendous volleys of musketry, hurling back line after line, only to be replaced by fresh assailants. Each moment the conflict became closer and more deadly. At times the roar of musketry gave place to the clash of bayonets, and at one point, after the Confederates had exhausted their ammunition, the assailants were repelled with stones which had been thrown up from a neighboring excavation. At the critical moment when the fate of Jackson's corps was trembling in the balance, Colonel Lee dashed with his artillery into a position that enfiladed the Federal right wing and hurled upon it a storm of shot and shell. At the same moment Longstreet's infantry rushed like a tempest against Pope's left, driving everything before it. This assault was irresistible, and speedily decided the fortune of the day. Pope's left wing gave way before it at every point, and his right, being assailed in flank and threatened in rear, relaxed its efforts and began to retire.

The Confederates, seeing the enemy in retreat, pursued with a shout that rose above the din of battle, and pressed him with such vigor that he soon fell into disorder and broke into rapid flight toward Bull Run. The pursuit was continued until arrested by the cover of night. After the storm of battle the field presened a scene of dreadful carnage. Thirty thousand men *hors de combat*, wrecks of batteries and the mangled carcasses of horses, gave proof of the desperate character of the conflict. Pope left upon the field 15,000 killed, wounded, and prisoners, while his army was greatly reduced by stragglers, who, imbued with the sentiment, "He who fights and runs away will live to fight another day," sought refuge far beyond the range of battle. The Confederate loss was also heavy, the killed and wounded being numbered at between 7000 and 8000. Beside the heavy losses in *personnel* sustained by the Federals, a large amount of valuable property fell into the hands of the victor, the most important of which was twenty-five thousand stand of small-arms and twenty-three pieces of artillery; also a large amount of medical stores was subsequently taken at Centreville.

Pope retired to Centreville, where he was opportunely joined by Generals Sumner and Franklin with 25,000 fresh troops, upon which Pope endeavored to rally his army.

General Lee, being well aware that powerful reinforcements from McClellan's and

BELOW: The dedication of a monument to the dead of First Bull Run in Virginia. Five times as many would die in the second campaign.

Burnside's armies and from other sources had been ordered to join Pope, did not deem it advisable to immediately pursue the retreating enemy, but prudently paused to ascertain what force he had to contend with before renewing the conflict. After the close of the battle Colonel Long made a personal reconnoissance of the whole field and reported to Lee. Wishing to strike the enemy another blow before he could recover from the effects of his repulse, Lee by rapid movement turned Centreville on the 1st of September, and took a position on the Little River turnpike, between Chantilly and Ox Hill, with the view of intercepting his retreat to Washington. This movement was covered by Robertson's cavalry, while Stuart advanced to Germantown, a small village a few miles east of Ox Hill, where he discovered the Federal army in retreat.

After a sharp attack Stuart was obliged to retire before a superior force. About dusk A. P. Hill's division encountered a large detachment of the enemy at Ox Hill. A brief but sanguinary combat ensued, ... The combatants being separated by night and storm, Hill's division occupied the field, while the Federals resumed the retreat. In this engagement they numbered among their slain two distinguished officers (Generals Kearny and Stephens), whose loss was regretted by friends in both armies. Pope made good his retreat during the night, and we once more see the fugitives from Manassas seeking a refuge within the defences of Washington.

* * *

Chapter III

Antietam

With the view of shedding additional light on this period of the history of the war, we shall here introduce a scrap of personal information. On the 2d of September succeeding Pope's defeat, Colonel Long wrote from the dictation of General Lee to President Davis in substance as follows: As Virginia was free from invaders, the Federal army being within the defences of Washington, shattered and dispirited by defeat, and as the passage of the Potomac could now be effected without opposition, the present was deemed a proper moment, with His Excellency's approbation, to penetrate into Maryland. The presence of the victorious army could not fail to alarm the Federal authorities and make them draw forces from every quarter for the defence of their capital, thus relieving the Confederacy from pressure and – for a time, at least – from the exhaustion incident to invasion. The presence of a powerful army would also revive the hopes of the Marylanders, allow them a free exercise of their sympathies, and give them an opportunity of rallying to the aid of their Southern friends. Above all, the position of the army, should it again be crowned with victory, would be most favorable for seizing and making the best use of the advantages which such an event would produce. In conclusion, a few remarks were made in regard to the condition of the army.

In anticipation of the President's concurrence, General Lee immediately began the preparation for the invasion of Maryland. On the 3d he put the army in motion, and on the 4th took a position between Leesburg and the contiguous fords of the Potomac. The inhabitants of this section of country, having been crushed by the heel of oppression, were now transported with the cheering prospect of liberty. The presence of the army whose movements they had anxiously and proudly watched filled them with unbounded joy. Their doors were thrown open and their stores were spread out in hospitable profusion to welcome their honored guest. Leesburg, being on the border, had at an early period fallen into the hands of the enemy. All of the men who were able had joined the army, and many of those who were unfit for service had retired within the Confederate lines to escape the miseries of the Northern prison; so that the women and children had been left almost alone. Now all these gladly returned to their homes, and tender greetings on every side penetrated to the deepest recesses of the heart and made them thank God that misery and woe had

BELOW: Residents of Sharpsburg, Maryland, flee the town at the approach of Confederate troops.

been replaced by happiness and joy.

The strength of the Confederate army at this time, including D. H. Hill's division, did not exceed 45,000 effective men; yet, though it had been greatly reduced in numbers during the campaign through which it had just passed, its spirit was raised by the victories it had achieved. Its numerical diminution was not so much the result of casualties in battle as that of losses incident to long and rapid marches with insufficient supplies of food and the want of shoes. It frequently happened that the only food of the soldiers was the green corn and fruit gathered from the fields and orchards adjacent to the line of march, and often the bravest men were seen with lacerated feet painfully striving to keep pace with their comrades, until, worn out with pain and fatigue, they were obliged to yield and wait to be taken up by the ambulances or wagons, to be carried where their wants could be supplied.

The invasion of Maryland being determined on, the army was stripped of all incumbrances, and, from fear that the soldiers might be induced to retaliate on the defenceless inhabitants for outrages committed by the Federal troops upon the people of the South, stringent orders were issued against straggling and plundering. These orders were strictly enforced throughout the campaign.

* * *

The passage of the Potomac was successfully accomplished on the 5th. The infantry, artillery, and trains crossed at White's and Cheek's fords, the cavalry having previously crossed with instructions to seize important points and cover the movements of the army. From the Potomac, General Lee advanced to Frederick, at which place he arrived on the 6th and established himself behind the Monocacy. He at the same time seized the Baltimore and Ohio Railroad, and the principal roads to Baltimore, Washington, Harper's Ferry, and the upper Potomac. From this important position radiated several lines upon which he could operate. Those toward Harper's Ferry, Baltimore, and

ABOVE: Stonewall Jackson's men wading across the Potomac at White's Ford.

Pennsylvania were unoccupied, while that in the direction of Washington was held by the Federal army.

* * *

It was not without surprise that General Lee discovered, upon reaching Frederick, that Harper's Ferry was still garrisoned. He had expected on entering Maryland that it would be at once abandoned, as it should have been had ordinary military principles been observed. Its continued occupation subjected its defenders to imminent danger of capture. Yet, through a military error, its occupation was unfavorable to the success of the Confederate movement, particularly if there was any idea entertained by General Lee of invading Pennsylvania. It would not do to leave this strongly-fortified post, on the direct line of communication of the army, in possession of the enemy; yet to reduce it needed a separation and retardation of the army that seriously interfered with the projected movements, and might have resulted adversely to the Southern cause but for the rapidity of Jackson's marches and the errors

of Colonel Miles, the commander of the garrison. This will appear when we come to describe the subsequent events.

Yet, whatever might be the effect, its reduction was absolutely necessary where any further operations of importance could be undertaken. Nor could the whole army be judiciously used for this purpose. Not only is it extremely unusual for a commander to use his whole force for a service which can be performed by a detachment, but in this case it would have necessitated a recrossing of the Potomac, with the strong probability that McClellan would take sure measures to prevent a return of the army into Maryland.

This service, had the claims of senior rank been alone considered, should have been intrusted to Longstreet; but it was given to Jackson on account of his superior qualifications for duty of this character, Longstreet making no objection. Jackson was therefore directed to move his corps on the morning of the 10th by way of Williamsport to Martinsburg, to capture or disperse the Federal force at that place, and then proceed to Harper's Ferry and take steps for its immediate reduction. At the same time, Major-general McLaws was ordered to move with his and Anderson's divisions by the most direct route upon Maryland Heights, to seize that important position and co-operate with Jackson in his attack on Harper's Ferry. Brigadier-general Walker was instructed to recross the Potomac with his division and occupy Loudoun Heights for the same purpose. The several movements were executed with wonderful celerity and precision.

Jackson on leaving Frederick marched with great rapidity by way of Middletown, Boonsboro', and Williamsport, near which latter place he forded the Potomac on the 11th and entered Virginia. Here he disposed his forces so as to prevent an escape of the garrison of Harper's Ferry in this direction and marched upon that place, the rear of which he reached on the 13th. On his approach General White evacuated Martinsburg and retired with its garrison to Harper's Ferry. On reaching Bolivar Heights, Jackson found that Walker was already the foot of Maryland Heights, the key to Harper's Ferry, since it is the loftiest of the three heights by which that place is surrounded, and is sufficiently near to reach it even by musketry. Harper's Ferry, in fact, is a mere trap for its garrison, since it lies open to cannonade

from the three heights named; so that the occupation of these renders it completely untenable.

Colonel Miles had posted a small force under Colonel Ford on Maryland Heights, retaining the bulk of his troops in Harper's

BELOW: Federal defenders on Maryland Heights, the point commanding Harper's Ferry. The position was abandoned quickly and reoccupied by Confederate troops on September 13.

Ferry. Instead of removing his whole command to the heights, which military prudence plainly dictated, and which his subordinates strongly recommended, he insisted upon a literal obedience to General Halleck's orders to hold Harper's Ferry to the last extremity. In fact, Maryland Heights was quickly abandoned altogether, Ford but feebly resisting McLaws and retiring before his advance, first spiking his guns and hurling them down the steep declivity. This retreat left Maryland Heights open to occupation by the assailing force, and it was not long ere McLaws had succeeded in dragging some guns to the summit of the rugged ridge and placing them in position to command the garrison below. Jackson and Walker were already in position, and, by the morning of the 14th, Harper's Ferry was completely invested. During the day the summits of the other hills were crowned with artillery, which was ready to open fire by dawn . . . .

There was never a more complete trap than that into which the doomed garrison had suffered itself to fall. Escape and resistance were alike impossible. Maryland Heights might easily have been held until McClellan came up had the whole garrison defended it, but its abandonment was a fatal movement. They lay at the bottom of a funnel-shaped opening commanded by a plunging fire from three directions and within reach of volleys of musketry from Maryland Heights. Two hours of cannonade sufficed to prove this, and at the end of that time Colonel Miles raised the white flag of surrender. The signal was not immediately perceived by the Confederates, who continued their fire, one of the shots killing the Federal commander. The force surrendered numbered between 11,000 and 12,000 men, while there fell into Jackson's hands 73 pieces of artillery, 13,000 stand of arms, 200 wagons, and a large quantity of military stores.

Pending the reduction of Harper's Ferry, General Lee moved by easy marches with two divisions of Longstreet's corps to the neighborhood of Hagerstown, leaving D. H. Hill with his division and a detachment of cavalry to serve as rear-guard, with instructions to hold the Boonsboro' pass of South Mountain. By taking a position between Williamsport and Hagerstown a junction could be easily effected with the troops operating against Harper's Ferry, and on the reduction of that place Lee would have a

secure line of communication through the Valley of Virginia, which would enable him to advance into Pennsylvania or to assume such other line of operation as circumstances might suggest.

Since the advance of the Confederate army into Maryland no considerable Federal force had appeared, and as yet only some unimportant cavalry affairs had occurred. After the evacuation of Virginia the Army of the Potomac had been augmented by the addition of the Army of Virginia and that of General Burnside, giving it an effective strength of about 90,000 men. This force was assigned to the command of General McClellan for active operations, and was put in motion about the 6th of September.

Although it was known in Washington that Lee had crossed the Potomac, McClellan was checked in his movements by General Halleck, who was still apprehensive that the ubiquitous Jackson or Stuart might suddenly appear before Washington.

When it became known that Lee had left Frederick and was advancing toward Hagerstown, McClellan advanced with greater

ABOVE: Union Major General Ambrose E. Burnside added his forces to McClellan's after the Federals evacuated Virginia.

OPPOSITE TOP: An abolitionist song inspired by the civil-rights activist Frederick Douglass, himself a former slave.

OPPOSITE BOTTOM: Map of troop positions and routes in the area of Harper's Ferry for the period from September 13 to 17.

confidence, and an attempt was made to relieve Harper's Ferry. Franklin was sent to force his way through Crampton's Pass, in the South Mountain range. This pass was defended by Mumford's cavalry, supported by a part of McLaws's division, under General Cobb, who had been sent back with three brigades under orders to hold Crampton's Pass until Harper's Ferry had surrendered, "even if he lost his last man in doing it." This pass is in the rear of, and but five miles from, Maryland Heights, and its occupation by the Federals would have seriously imperilled the Confederate operations. It was gallantly defended against the strong force of assailants, and, though Franklin succeeded in forcing his way through by the morning of the 15th, he was too late: Miles was already on the point of surrender. McLaws at once withdrew his force from Maryland Heights, with the exception of one regiment, and formed a line of battle across Pleasant Valley to resist the threatening corps. The surrender of the garrison immediately afterward left him a free line of retreat. He crossed the Potomac at the Ferry, and moved by way of Shepherdstown to rejoin Lee at Sharpsburg. The Confederates had in this enterprise met with the most complete and gratifying success.

The Federal army, moving with great caution and deliberation, reached Frederick on the 12th. Here occurred one of those un-

BELOW: Confederate Brigadier General Howell Cobb of Georgia successfully defended a pass to Maryland Heights until the surrender of Harper's Ferry.

toward events which have so often changed the course of wars, and which in this instance completely modified the character of the campaign. A copy of General Lee's order directing the movements of the army accidentally fell into the hands of McClellan, who, being thus accurately informed of the position of the forces of his opponent, at once determined to abandon his cautious policy and boldly assume the offensive. He therefore pressed forward with the view of forcing the South Mountain passes, held by Hill, and of intruding himself between the wings of the Confederate army, with the hope of being able to crush them in detail before they could reunite.

The order in question, addressed to D. H. Hill, was found by a soldier after the Confederate evacuation of Frederick, and was quickly in McClellan's possession. Hill has been blamed for unpardonable carelessness in losing it; yet, as the original order was still in his possession after the war, it is evident that the one found must have been a copy. The mystery is made clear by Colonel Venable, one of General Lee's staff-officers, in the following remark: "This is very easily explained. One copy was sent directly to Hill from headquarters. General Jackson sent him a copy, as he regarded Hill in his command. It is Jackson's copy, in his own handwriting, which General Hill has. The other was undoubtedly left carelessly by some one at Hill's headquarters." However that be, its possession by McClellan immediately reversed the character of his movements, which were changed from snail-like slowness to energetic rapidity. In his own words, "Upon learning the contents of this order, I at once gave orders for a vigorous pursuit."

The detachment by General Lee of a large portion of his army for the reduction of Harper's Ferry was made with the reasonable assurance that that object could be effected and a junction formed before General McClellan would be in position to press him. Though this expectation proved well based, yet it was imperilled by the unforeseen event above mentioned.

The rapid movements to which the finding of Lee's order gave rise brought the leading corps of the Federal army in front of Hill's position upon South Mountain on the afternoon of the 13th. This mountain is intersected by three passes in front of Boonsboro'. The main, or central, pass is traversed by the Frederick and Boonsboro' turnpike; the second, three-fourths of a mile south-east of the first, is crossed by the old Sharpsburg turnpike; the third is an obscure pass behind the elevated crest, about a quarter of a mile north-west of the turnpike.

General Hill's right occupied the southeast pass, and his left held the central. The centre was posted on a narrow mountain-road connecting the right and left. The pass on the left was watched by a small cavalry force. The position of Hill was strong, as it was only assailable by the pike on the left and the road on the right and along the rugged mountain-sides.

Early on the morning of the 14th, General McClellan advanced to the attack, directing his principal efforts against the south-east pass. Hill maintained his position with his usual firmness and intrepidity, and his troops exhibited the same gallantry that had characterized them on various fields.

At this time the position of the several corps of the Confederate army was the following: Jackson was at Harper's Ferry, about fifteen miles from Sharpsburg; Longstreet, at Hagerstown, a somewhat greater distance to the north of Sharpsburg; and D. H. Hill, at Boonsboro' Gap, eastward of these positions; while McClellan's whole force, with the exception of the detachment sent toward Harper's Ferry, lay east of the Gap. Had the Gap been left undefended, as it has been recently suggested it should have been, there would have been nothing to hinder McClellan from inserting his army between the two sections of the Confederate forces and attacking them in detail. The occupation of Sharpsburg by the enemy would have placed Lee in a difficult and dangerous position. Had he retired across the Potomac, as it has been suggested was

ABOVE: General McClellan's headquarters guard, the New York 93rd Volunteers, gathers at Antietam for a photograph by Alexander Gardner, one of photographer Mathew B. Brady's staff, on September 16, 1862.

his proper course to pursue, it would have been a virtual abandonment of his trains and artillery, which were then extended along the road between Hagerstown and Sharpsburg, and could have been reached by McClellan with his cavalry in an hour or two from Boonsboro'.

The battle of Boonsboro' was therefore necessary to the security of the army; and when, on the night of the 13th, Lee received information of the rapid advance of McClellan, he at once took steps for the effective reinforcement of General Hill. Longstreet's corps was put in motion for this purpose early in the morning of the 14th, and, fortunately, arrived at the Gap in time to prevent Hill's brave men from being overwhelmed by the superior numbers of the enemy.

This timely reinforcement secured the Confederate position. McClellan, finding that his efforts against the centre and right were unavailing, at length discontinued them, with the intention of renewing the

conflict at a more assailable point. The contest during the morning had been severe and the loss on each side considerable. On the side of the Confederates, the chief loss fell on the brigade of Brigadier-general Garland. This brigade numbered among its slain its gallant commander, who fell while bravely opposing a fierce attack on South-east Pass.

When General Lee reached Boonsboro' with Longstreet's corps, he sent forward Colonel Long, Major Venable, and other members of his staff, to learn the condition of affairs in front. The pass on the left proved to be unoccupied, and a heavy Federal force was tending in that direction. In anticipation of an attack from this quarter, Hood's division was deployed across the turnpike and Rodes's was posted on the ridge overlooking the unoccupied pass, with Evans's brigade connecting his right with Hood's left. There was a small field in front of Evans and Hood, while Rodes was masked by the timber on the side of the mountain. About three

BELOW: Union scouts and guides for the Army for the Potomac photographed in October 1862 by Alexander Gardner.

o'clock the battle was renewed by McClellan, who with great energy directed his main attack against Rodes. This was successfully resisted until nightfall, when Rodes's troops gave way before the assault of a superior force. The possession of the ground that had been held by Rodes gave the Federals the command of the central pass, but they could not immediately avail themselves of their success, on account of the . . . darkness.

The Confederate position was now untenable, and its evacuation became necessary. The withdrawal of the rear-guard was assigned to General Rodes, the successful execution of the movement being in a great measure due to the sagacity and boldness of Major Green Peyton, adjutant-general of Rodes's division.

At ten o'clock the next morning the Confederate army was safely in position at Sharpsburg.

At Boonsboro', McClellan had displayed more than usual pertinacity in his attacks

LEFT: Confederate Major General James Longstreet opposed Lee's choice of Sharpsburg as the battle site. At the battle, his men formed Lee's right, anchored at Antietam Creek.

BELOW: The Boonesborough Pike crossing at Antietam Bridge in September 1862.

strong and much better field than that of the previous day. He remained in his new position during the 18th, prepared for battle; but General McClellan, perceiving that his troops had been greatly disorganized by the battle of the previous day, declined resuming the attack until the arrival of 15,000 fresh troops that were hastening to his support.

Foreseeing that no important results could be achieved by a second battle with McClellan's augmented forces, and being unwilling to sacrifice unnecessarily his gallant men, Lee withdrew during the night to the south side of the Potomac, and on the 19th took a position a few miles west of Shepherdstown.

When McClellan learned, on the morning of the 19th, that the Confederate position had been evacuated, he ordered an immediate pursuit, which, however, proved unavailing, as the Confederate rear-guard was disappearing in the defile leading from the ford below Shepherdstown when the Federal advance appeared on the opposite heights. A few batteries were then put into position, and a harmless cannonade commenced, which was kept up in a desultory manner during the greater part of the day. Late in the afternoon a large detachment approached the ford, and about nightfall dislodged General Pendleton, who had been charged with its defence, and effected a

BELOW: On October 4 President Lincoln went to the Antietam battlefield to try personally to persuade General McClellan to pursue General Lee. The Union general, however, would not cross the Potomac River into Virginia until October 26.

crossing without serious opposition. This occurrence was reported about midnight to General Lee, who immediately despatched orders to Jackson to take steps to arrest the Federal advance. The division of A. P. Hill, moving with rapidity, reached the mouth of the defile leading to the river just as the Federal detachment was debouching from it, and attacked this force with such impetuosity that it was compelled to retire with heavy loss across the Potomac. McClellan made no further attempt to continue offensive operations for several weeks, this interval being passed in the neighborhood of Sharpsburg in resting and reorganizing his forces. This campaign, especially the battle of Sharpsburg, has been the subject of much discussion, in which the Northern writers generally claim for the Federal arms a complete victory; but the historian of the Army of the Potomac, with greater impartiality, acknowledges Antietam (or Sharpsburg) to have been a drawn battle. This admission is corroborated by the evidence of General McClellan in his testimony before the Congressional Committee on the Conduct of the War, since he admitted that his losses on the 17th had been so heavy, and that his forces were so greatly disorganized on the morning of the 18th, that, although General Lee still maintained a defiant attitude, he was unable to resume the attack. Swinton, however, claims for the Army of the Potomac a political victory, with apparent justice; but in reality his claim is without foundation, for Lee was politically defeated before the occurrence of a collision with McClellan by his failure to induce the Marylanders to rally in any considerable force to his standard; and even when McClellan, by accident, became aware of the disposition of his forces and his intentions, he was establishing a line of communication that would enable him to engage his opponent with no other hope of political results than such as would naturally arise from a victory, whether gained north or south of the Potomac. The severe chastisement that had been inflicted on the Army of the Potomac is evident from the long prostration it exhibited, notwithstanding the facility with which it received reinforcements and supplies.

ABOVE: Lincoln at Antietam with General McClellan. From left they are: Gen. G. W. Morell, Col. A. S. Webb, McClellan, scout Adams, Dr. J. Letterman, an unidentified officer, Lincoln, Col. H. J. Hunt, and Gen. Fitz John Porter.

Chapter IV

Fredericksburg

After remaining a few days in the neighborhood of Shepherdstown, General Lee gradually withdrew to a position between Bunker Hill and Winchester. Notwithstanding he had failed, from accidental causes, to accomplish the chief object of the invasion of Maryland, the expedition was not wholly without beneficial results, since it relieved Virginia from the presence of the enemy and gave her an opportunity to recover in a measure from the exhausting effect of war . . . .

* * *

The inactivity of General McClellan allowed General Lee several weeks of uninterrupted repose. During that interval the guardianship of the Potomac was confided to the cavalry and horse-artillery. While thus employed General Stuart made a swoop into Pennsylvania, captured a thousand horses, and after making the entire circuit of the Federal army recrossed the Potomac with only the loss of three missing . . . .

Throughout the late campaign the duty of selecting a place for headquarters usually devolved upon the writer. The general would say, "Colonel Long has a good eye for locality: let him find a place for the camp." It was not always so easy to find a desirable situation, but, as the general was easily satisfied, the difficulties of the task were greatly lightened. Only once, to my recollection, did he object to the selection made for headquarters; this was on reaching the neighborhood of Winchester. The army had preceded the general and taken possession of every desirable camping-place. After a long and fatiguing search a farm-house was discovered, surrounded by a large shady yard. The occupants of the house with great satisfaction gave permission for the establishment of General Lee not only in the yard, but insisted on his occupying a part of the house. Everything being satisfactorily settled, the wagons were ordered up, but just as their unloading began the general rode up and flatly refused to occupy either

yard or house. No one expected him to violate his custom by occupying the house, but it was thought he would not object to a temporary occupation of the yard. Being vexed at having to look for another place for headquarters, I ordered the wagons into a field almost entirely covered with massive stones. The boulders were so large and thick that it was difficult to find space for the tents. The only redeeming feature the location possessed was a small stream of good water. When the tents were pitched, the general looked around with a smile of satisfaction, and said, "This is better than the yard. We will not now disturb those good people."

While occupying this camp we were visited by several distinguished British officers – among them, Colonel Garnet Wolseley, who has since become prominent in history. Subsequently, one of the number published the following account of General Lee and his surroundings:

In visiting the headquarters of the Confederate generals, but particularly those of General Lee, any one accustomed to see

European armies in the field, cannot fail to be struck with the great absence of all the pomp and circumstance of war in and around their encampments.

Lee's headquarters consisted of about seven or eight poletents, pitched, with their backs to a stake-fence, upon a piece of ground so rocky that it was unpleasant to ride over it, its only recommendation being a little stream of good water which flowed close by the general's tent. In front of the tents were some three or four army-wagons, drawn up without any regularity, and a number of horses turned loose about the field. The servants – who were, of course, slaves – and the mounted soldiers called couriers, who always accompany each general of division in the field, were unprovided with tents, and slept in or under the wagons. Wagons, tents, and some of the horses were marked "U.S.," showing that part of that huge debt in the North has gone to furnishing even the Confederate generals with camp-equipments. No guard or sentries were to be seen in the vicinity, no crowd of aides-de-camp loitering about, making themselves agreeable to visitors and endeavoring to save their generals from receiving those who had no particular business. A large farm-house stands close by, which in any other army would have been the general's residence *pro tem*.; but, as no liberties are allowed to be taken with personal property in Lee's army, he is particular in setting a good example himself. His staff are crowded together, two or three in a

BELOW: A group of European officers who visited troops in the field near Yorktown, Va. in May 1862.

ABOVE: A Confederate camp in autumn.

RIGHT: Soldier drawing water for a hospital at Fredericksburg.

tent; none are allowed to carry more baggage than a small box each, and his own kit is but very little larger. Every one who approaches him does so with marked respect, although there is none of that bowing and flourishing of forage-caps which occurs in the presence of European generals; and, while all honor him and place implicit faith in his courage and ability, those with whom he is most intimate feel for him the affection of sons to a father. Old General Scott was correct in saying that when Lee joined the Southern cause it was worth as much as the accession of 20,000 men to the "rebels." Since then every injury that it was possible to inflict the Northerners have heaped upon him. Notwithstanding all these personal losses, however, when speaking of the Yankees he neither evinced any bitterness of feeling nor gave utterance to a single violent expression, but alluded to many of his former friends and companions among them in the kindest terms. He spoke as a man proud of the victories won by his country and confident of ultimate success

under the blessing of the Almighty, whom he glorified for past successes, and whose aid he invoked for all future operations.

Notwithstanding the ruggedness of this encampment, it proved unusually lively. Besides the foreign friends, we had numerous visitors from the army, also ladies and gentlemen from Winchester and the neighborhood, all of whom had some remark to make upon the rocky situation of our camp. This the general seemed to enjoy, as it gave him an opportunity of making a jest at the expense of Colonel Long, whom he accused of having set him down there among the rocks in revenge for his refusing to occupy the yard. Although there were no habitual drinkers on the general's staff, an occasional demijohn would find its way to headquarters. While at this place one of the officers received a present of a jug of fine old rye. Soon after its advent General J. E. B. Stuart, with Sweeney and his banjo, arrived – not on account, however, of the jug, but, as was his wont, to give us a serenade. The

ABOVE: Building a stockade at Alexandria, Virginia.

ABOVE: Night amusements around a Confederate campfire.

bright camp-fire was surrounded by a merry party, and a lively concert commenced. After a while the general came out, and, observing the jug perched on a boulder, asked with a merry smile, "Gentlemen, am I to thank General Stuart or the jug for this fine music?"

By this time the men had come to know their leader. The brilliant campaigns through which he had led them had inspired them with love and confidence, and whenever he appeared among them his approach was announced by "Here comes Mars' Robert!" and he would be immediately saluted with the well-known Confederate yell, which called forth in other quarters the exclamation, "There goes Mars' Robert – ole Jackson, or an ole hare."

*　　*　　*

The repose of a month had greatly improved in every way the Confederate army; it had reached a high state of efficiency, and General Lee was fully prepared to meet General McClellan whenever he might think fit to advance to attack him in his position

before Winchester. When McClellan . . . had crossed the Potomac and the direction of his advance was ascertained, Lee moved Longstreet's corps and the greater part of the cavalry to a position near Culpeper Court-house and established his outposts along the right bank of the Rappahannock. Jackson's corps was detained in the Valley until the Federal plans should be more fully developed.

The delay that followed the battle of Sharpsburg and the deliberate manner in which McClellan resumed active operations . . . were productive of a voluminous correspondence with Mr. Lincoln and General Halleck, . . . which culminated in the removal of McClellan . . . .

*　　*　　*

A great diversity of opinion exists as to the military capacity of McClellan, and he has been both unduly praised and censured by his friends and foes. That his slowness and caution were elements on which the opposing general might safely count must be admitted, but that he had a high degree of military ability cannot be denied. His skill in planning movements was certainly admirable, but their effect was in more than one instance lost by over-slowness in their execution. In this connection it will be of interest to give General Lee's own opinion concerning McClellan's ability, as related by a relative of the general, who had it from her father, an old gentleman of eighty years:

"One thing I remember hearing him say. He asked General Lee which in his opinion was the ablest of the Union generals; to which the latter answered, bringing his hand down on the table with an emphatic energy, 'McClellan, by all odds!'"

This opinion, however, could but have referred to his skill as a tactician, as it is unquestionable that Lee availed himself of McClellan's over-caution and essayed perilous movements which he could not have safely ventured in the presence of a more active opponent.

It was with surprise that the Confederate officers who knew the distinguished merit of Sumner, Sedgwick, Meade, and others learned that Burnside had been elevated above them, and General Burnside himself with diffidence accepted the high honor that had been conferred upon him. Mr. Lincoln, accompanied by General Halleck, visited the headquarters of the army near Warrenton, where a plan of operations was adopted. A rapid advance upon Richmond by the way of Fredericksburg was advised. It was supposed from the position of General Lee's forces that by gaining a march or two upon him Richmond might be reached and captured before that general could relieve it. All that prevented the immediate execution of this plan was the want of a pontoon-train, which was necessary for the passage of the Rappahannock.

Having arranged to his satisfaction with General Halleck and Mr. Lincoln in regard to a prompt compliance with his requisitions for pontoons and supplies for the army, General Burnside, about the 15th of November, put the Army of the Potomac in motion, and on the 17th, Sumner's corps reached Fredericksburg. This energetic officer would probably have immediately crossed the Rappahannock by the fords above the town, and

ABOVE: Union General Meade (fourth from right) and General Sedgwick (second from right) were both considered more able than Major General Burnside, whom Lincoln chose to elevate over them as commander of the Army of the Potomac.

ABOVE: A Federal cavalry column forms up near a pontoon bridge after crossing the Rappahannock.

RIGHT: Federal earthworks on the north bank of the North Anna River facing Confederate earthworks in the distance.

OPPOSITE TOP: Three Confederate pickets at Fredericksburg.

OPPOSITE BOTTOM: Union pontoon wagons on the way to Burnside in December.

Brigadier-general Ransom, occupied the reverse slope of the heights. [These troops did good service during the battle.] On the hills behind were grouped batteries so disposed that the heights in front could be raked with shot and shell in case they were carried by the Federals.

On the morning of the 13th of December, as the fog slowly lifted, a scene was unfolded which in point of grandeur has seldom been witnessed. The Stafford Heights, from Falmouth to the Massaponax, were crowned with thickly-grouped batteries of artillery, while the shores of the Rappahannock were

ABOVE: Union artillery used to soften Confederate resistance at Fredericksburg.

covered with dark masses of troops in battle array. Opposite the Confederate right the attacking force, in two lines, began to advance. Simultaneously the heights were wreathed in smoke and the thunder of artillery announced the commencement of battle. When the attacking column had become disengaged from the embankments of the river-road, Stuart's horse artillery on the right and the artillery of Jackson's corps in front opened a destructive fire, which checked it for a brief space, until its own batteries could be placed in position to occupy the opposing artillery. It then moved steadily onward, and quickly dislodged the first Confederate line from the railroad, and disappeared in the wood that concealed the greater part of the second line. A deadly conflict ensued, which, although hidden by the forest, was proclaimed by the terrific clash of musketry. Very soon the troops that had advanced so gallantly were seen to retire. At first a straggling few and then large masses came rushing out, followed by long lines of gray veterans, who dealt death at every step.

General Meade, from the want of support after his gallant achievement, was compelled to witness the present deplorable condition of his corps. Forty thousand of Franklin's grand division, remaining idly by, had beheld the defeat of their brave comrades without extending a helping hand. This apathy of Franklin was at the time regarded by the Confederates as remarkable.

During the attack on the right preparations were in progress to assail the Confederate centre. Dense masses of troops, which had been previously concentrated in and about Fredericksburg, were now formed in columns of attack to be led against Marye's Heights. About noon the attack commenced. Column after column advanced to the assault, to be hurled back with terrible slaughter. Attack after attack was hopelessly renewed until the stoutest heart quailed at the dreadful carnage that ensued. Seeing his repeated efforts unavailing, General Burnside ordered a discontinuance of the conflict. The Confederates on the next day expected the battle to be renewed with greater vigor than had been displayed on the day before, but the Federals maintained a sullen silence, and at night recrossed the Rappahannock. The next morning the spectator could hardly believe his senses on beholding the great Federal army that had on the day previous lined the southern shore of the Rappahannock now covering the heights of Stafford, bereft of that martial spirit it had exhibited a few days before. The dispirited condition of the Federal army was not so much the consequence of losses in battle as the effect of the want of co-operation and the fruitless results of misdirected valor.

The appointment of General Burnside to the command of the Army of the Potomac had proved a mistake – more, however, from the combination of circumstances against him than from lack of conduct on his part. His successes in North Carolina had given him prominence, while his soldierly bearing and fine appearance evidently had their influence with Mr. Lincoln in the selection of him as commander-in-chief of the Army of the Potomac, while neglecting the superior claims of several others, two of whom – Generals Hooker and Franklin – could never forget their sense of superiority sufficiently to render him cordial co-operation. Bour-

BELOW: War artist A. R. Waud's on-the-scene sketch of Union soldiers building the pontoon bridge of the Rappahannock to attack Fredericksburg.

rienne gives us a maxim of Bonaparte that "two great generals in the same army are sure to make a bad one." This maxim particularly applied in the present instance to the Army of the Potomac, where its truth was fully verified.

The losses sustained, as stated by General Burnside, amounted to about 10,000, among whom was General Bayard, a young officer of great merit, whose loss was sincerely felt in the army as well as by a large circle of acquaintances. The Confederate loss was numerically much less than that sustained by the enemy. The Confederates, however, numbered among their slain Brigadier-generals Gregg and Cobb, and among their mortally wounded Colonel Coleman of the artillery. The fall of these noble and gallant spirits was deeply deplored by the army.

*　　*　　*

After the battle of Fredericksburg, General Lee retained his headquarters, established previous to the battle, at a point on the road midway between Fredericksburg and Hamilton Crossing, selected on account of its accessibility. Although there was a vacant house near which he could have occupied, he preferred . . . to remain in camp, thus giving an example of endurance of hardship that might prove useful to his troops

*　　*　　*

OPPOSITE: Confederate dead behind the stone wall at the foot of Marye's Heights, from behind which Longstreet's infantry poured deadly fire on the Union attackers.

BELOW: Fredericksburg viewed from the river. Rebel troops stand on what remains of the town's wrecked bridge.

Chapter V

Chancellorsville

The Army of Northern Virginia in the winter of 1862-63 began to feel seriously the want of . . . money and men. The Army of Northern Virginia was deficient in clothing, shoes, blankets, tents, provisions; in fact, everything needful was wanted except arms and ammunition . . . In order to relieve the drain upon the scanty commissariat, Longstreet was sent with two divisions to the district south of Petersburg, where provisions were still abundant, with a view of subsisting these troops, while they collected the surplus supplies to be sent to the troops in other quarters. This detachment reduced the Confederate army to barely 40,000 men, while the Federal force exceeded 100,000.

After this reduction General Lee conceived the design of adopting a position more remote from the Federal lines than the one he then occupied, . . . [but as] no position could be found which afforded greater advantages than the one he then occupied, Lee continued to hold the line of the Rappahannock, and busied himself in preparation for the ensuing campaign.

*   *   *

The appointment of Hooker to the command of the Army of the Potomac was a surprise to General Lee, who had no great respect for the military ability of his new opponent in a position of such importance. Swinton thus comments on the condition of the Army of the Potomac and the appointment of Hooker to the supreme command:

Notwithstanding the untoward fortunes the Army of the Potomac had suffered, it could hardly be said to be really demoralized, for

BELOW: By winter of 1862-63 the South began to grow short of materiel to support the war. Confederate soldiers are shown stripping clothing and boots from fallen Union soldiers.

its heart was still in the war; it never failed to respond to any demand made upon it; and it was ever ready to renew its courage at the first ray of hope. Such a day-spring came with the appointment of General Hooker to the chief command, and under his influence the tone of the army underwent a change that would appear astonishing had not its elastic vitality been so often proved. Hooker's measures of reform were judicious: he cut away the roots of many evils; stopped desertion and its causes; did away with the nuisance of the "grand-division" organization; infused vitality through the staff and administrative service; gave distinctive badges to the different corps; instituted a system of furloughs; consolidated the cavalry under able leaders, and soon enabled it not only to stand upon an equality with, but to assert its superiority over, the Virginia horsemen of Stuart. These things proved General Hooker to be an able administrative officer, but they did not prove him to be a competent commander for a great army, and whatever anticipation might be formed touching this had to be drawn from his previous career as a corps commander, in which he had won the reputation of being what is called a "dashing" officer, and carried the sobriquet of "Fighting Joe."

The new commander judiciously resolved to defer all grand military operations during the wet season, and the first three months after he assumed command were well spent in rehabilitating the army. The ranks were filled up by the return of absentees; the discipline and instruction of the troops were energetically continued; and the close of April found the Army of the Potomac in a high degree of efficiency in all arms. It numbered 120,000 men (infantry and artillery), with a body of 12,000 well-equipped cavalry and a powerful artillery force of above 400 guns. It was divided into seven corps – the First corps under General Reynolds; the Second under General Couch; the Third under General Sickles; the Fifth under General Meade; the Sixth under General Sedgwick; the Eleventh under General Howard; and the Twelfth under General Slocum.

During his period of preparation Hooker very properly resisted that spirit of impa-

ABOVE: Union General Joseph ("Fighting Joe") Hooker, who rehabilitated the Army of the Potomac in the winter 1862-63.

best disciplined, the most high-spirited, and enthusiastic army on the continent. It consisted of 52,000 infantry, 250 pieces of artillery, and 9000 cavalry, making an aggregate force of 65,000 men. The successful campaign which this army had recently passed through inspired it with almost invincible ardor. This splendid result had been accomplished by the almost unaided efforts of General Lee.

* * *

ABOVE: A stone marker at the spot where General Jackson fell.

LEFT: Enlistees departing near Falmouth, Virginia, after the Chancellorsville campaign.

Chapter VI

Gettysburg

By the first of June General Lee had completed his arrangements for the ensuing campaign. The army, though numerically less than it was when he commenced his operations against McClellan on the Chickahominy, had been by its recent victories imbued with a confidence that greatly increased its efficiency. Its spirit was now high, and it was anxious to grapple again its powerful foe, which still lingered on the Stafford Heights.

The object of the campaign being the defence of Richmond, General Lee could either continue on the defensive and oppose the Federal advance as he had recently done, or he might assume the offensive and by bold manoeuvring oblige the Federal army to recede from its present line of operations to protect its capital or oppose the invasion of Maryland or Pennsylvania.

The advance upon Richmond would thus be frustrated, and the attack upon that city delayed, at least for a time. The dispirited condition of the Federal army since its late defeat, and the high tone of that of the Confederates, induced the adoption of the latter plan.

This decision was reached by General Lee near the close of May and after the completion of the reorganization of the army which followed the battle of Chancellorsville. Before the movement began his plans of operation were fully matured, and with such precision that the exact locality at which a conflict with the enemy was expected to take place was indicated on his map. This locality was the town of Gettysburg, the scene of the subsequent great battle.

At the period mentioned he called the

BELOW: General Hooker's army marching past Manassas, Va. in June 1863. General Lee rejected suggestions that he engage the Army of the Potomac here.

writer into his tent, headquarters being then near Fredericksburg. On entering I found that he had a map spread on the table before him, which he seemed to have been earnestly consulting. He advised me of his designed plan of operations, which we discussed together and commented upon the probable result. He traced on the map the proposed route of the army and its destination in Pennsylvania, while in his quietly effective manner he made clear to me his plans for the campaign. He first proposed, in furtherance of his design, to manoeuvre the army in such a way as to draw Hooker from the Rappahannock. At this point in the conversation I suggested that it might be advantageous to bring Hooker to an engagement somewhere in the vicinity of the old battlefield of Manassas. To this idea General Lee objected, and stated as his reason for opposing it that no results of decisive value to the Confederate States could come from a victory in that locality. The Federal army, if defeated, would fall back to the defences of Washington, as on previous occasions, where it could reorganize in safety and again take the field in full force.

In his view, the best course would be to invade Pennsylvania, penetrating this State in the direction of Chambersburg, York, or Gettysburg. He might be forced to give battle at one or the other of these places as circumstances might suggest, but, in his view, the vicinity of Gettysburg was much the best point, as it was less distant from his base on the Potomac, and was so situated that by holding the passes of the South Mountain he would be able to keep open his line of communication. York, being some twenty-five miles farther from the mountains, was a less desirable locality.

In this plan he had a decided object. There was in his mind no thought of reaching Philadelphia, as was subsequently feared in the North. Yet he was satisfied that the Federal army, if defeated in a pitched battle, would be seriously disorganized and forced to retreat across the Susquehanna – an event which would give him control of Maryland and Western Pennsylvania, and probably of West Virginia, while it would very likely cause the fall of Washington City and the flight of the Federal Government. Moreover, an important diversion would be

ABOVE: Union cavalrymen of the 3rd Pennsylvannia, commanded by Alfred Pleasonton, photographed at Gettysburg.

made in favor of the Western department, where the affairs of the Confederacy were on the decline. These highly important results, which would in all probability follow a successful battle, fully warranted, in his opinion, the hazard of an invasion of the North.

The plan which he thus indicated was already fully matured in his own mind, and the whole line of movement was laid down on the map. He alluded to the several strategic points in Maryland, but did not think it would be advisable to make any stand in that State, for the same reason as before given. This interview took place about two weeks before the movement began. The proposed scheme of operations was submitted to President Davis in a personal interview, and fully approved by him.

* * *

On the 2d of June, Ewell's corps, preceded by the cavalry, was sent forward to Culpeper Court-house. A day or two after, Longstreet, accompanied by the commander-in-chief, followed Ewell, while Hill remained at Fredericksburg to observe the movements of Hooker. By the 8th of June

the main body of the Confederate army was concentrated in the neighborhood of Culpeper and the Federal army was in motion for the upper Rappahannock. . . . On the 10th, Ewell was advanced toward the Shenandoah Valley, both for the purpose of expelling from that section a considerable Federal force, and to create an impression of a flank movement with the view of interrupting Hooker's communications. . . . Hooker suddenly withdrew from the Rappahannock and retired to the vicinity of Manassas and Centreville, where he assumed a defensive attitude for the protection of Washington. Thus by a series of bold strategic movements General Lee removed the enemy from his path and accomplished the . . . extension of his line from Fredericksburg to Winchester in the face of an enemy of more than double his numerical strength.

*   *   *

On the 15th, Longstreet was put in motion for the Valley, and Hill was directed to follow a day later, . . . General Lee arrived with Longstreet's corps at Berryville on the 18th, . . . About the 21st he continued his advance in two columns: the one, composed of the corps of Ewell and Hill, was directed to Shepherdstown, and the other, consisting of Longstreet's corps and the supply-train, proceeded to Williamsport. Ewell crossed the Potomac on the 23d, followed by Hill on the 24th, while its passage was effected by Longstreet and the trains on the 25th at Williamsport.

As Lee's plan of operations unfolded itself, Hooker advanced to the Potomac and took possession of the fords in the neighborhood of Leesburg. When he learned that Lee had entered Maryland he immediately crossed the river and advanced to Frederick. A controversy then occurred between Halleck and himself, which resulted in his removal on the 27th and the placing of General Meade in command of the Army of the Potomac.

*   *   *

Immediately on completing the passage of the Potomac, Lee resumed his advance, directing Ewell to Carlisle, while he proceeded with Longstreet and Hill to Chambersburg. Ewell sent Early to York by way of Gettysburg, and then moved with the rest of his corps, accompanied by Jenkins's cavalry, to Carlisle. . . . Such was the disposition of the Confederate army during the latter part of June.

*   *   *

Lee first learned of the appointment of General Meade to the command of the Federal army on the 28th of June. . . . On reaching Chambersburg, General Lee . . . was

BELOW: Artillery going into action on the south bank of the Rappahannock on June 4.

ABOVE: War council of General Meade and his officers before the Battle of Gettysburg.

OPPOSITE TOP: The death of General John F. Reynolds, Commander of the Federal I Corps, on June 1.

OPPOSITE BOTTOM: Map of the three-day Battle of Gettysburg.

under the impression that the Federal army had not yet crossed the Potomac. It was not until the night of the 28th that he learned that the enemy had reached Frederick. . . .

The rapid advance of General Meade was unexpected, and exhibited a celerity that had not hitherto been displayed by the Federal army. A speedy concentration of the Confederate army was now necessary. Before dawn on the morning of the 29th orders were despatched requiring the immediate junction of the army, and on the 30th the Confederate forces were in motion toward Gettysburg. At the same time General Meade was pressing forward for that place.

This movement of the Confederate army began with the advance of A. P. Hill's corps, which bivouacked near Greenville on the night of the 29th, and reached Cashtown during the next day. Orders had been sent to Ewell to recall his advanced divisions and concentrate in the same locality. Longstreet's corps followed on the 30th, accompanied by headquarters, and encamped that night near the western base of South Mountain, in the neighborhood of the Stevens furnace. On July 1st he advanced to

Cashtown, a locality about six miles from Gettysburg.

While Lee and his staff were ascending South Mountain firing was heard from the direction of Gettysburg. This caused Lee some little uneasiness. The unfortunate absence of the cavalry prevented him from knowing the position and movements of the enemy, and it was impossible to estimate the true condition of affairs in his front. He was at first persuaded that the firing indicated a cavalry affair of minor importance, but by the time Cashtown was reached the sound had become heavy and continuous, and indicated a severe engagement.

General Lee now exhibited a degree of anxiety and impatience, and expressed regret at the absence of the cavalry. He said that he had been kept in the dark ever since crossing the Potomac, and intimated that Stuart's disappearance had materially hampered the movements and disorganized the plans of the campaign.

In a short time, however, his suspense was relieved by a message from A. P. Hill, who reported that he was engaged with two corps of the enemy, and requested reinforcements. Anderson's division, which had just reached Cashtown, was at once pushed forward to his support, and General Lee with his staff quickly followed.

The situation in front at that time was as follows: During the forenoon of July 1st the two leading corps of the Federal army, commanded by General Reynolds, had arrived at Gettysburg; at the same time the heads of Hill's and Ewell's corps were rapidly approaching. About ten o'clock, General Heth of Hill's corps encountered a part of Buford's cavalry, which had been thrown forward on the Chambersburg road to a small stream called Willoughby Run, three miles from Gettysburg. Having driven back Buford, Heth engaged Wadsworth's division of the First corps, which was soon reinforced by other divisions of that corps, while Heth was supported by Pender's division of Hill's corps. The advance of the Eleventh corps (Howard's) and the arrival of Rodes's and Early's divisions of Ewell's corps, increased the proportions of the combat, which quickly became animated and continued with spirit until about four o'clock in the afternoon, when the Federal corps were totally defeated and driven from the field with very heavy loss. General Reynolds was killed, and his two corps were seriously reduced in numbers and greatly disorganized. The Confederate loss was much

303

ABOVE: A scene of carnage at the three-day Battle of Gettysburg, July 1863.

smaller than that of the enemy; nevertheless, the fall of many gallant soldiers was to be regretted. Among the wounded was the gallant General Heth, whose command suffered severely.

Near the close of the action General Lee reached the field. Anderson's division came up soon afterward, and about the same time Longstreet arrived in advance of his corps, which was a few miles behind. As the troops were evidently very much fatigued, and somewhat disorganized by rapid marching and hard fighting, it seemed inadvisable to immediately pursue the advantage which had been gained, particularly as the retreating forces of the enemy were known to have been reinforced, and to have taken a defensive position about a mile south of the town.

This subject occupied Lee's attention upon perceiving the situation of affairs and the victory gained by his advance forces, and he entered into a conversation with Longstreet, in the presence of the writer, concerning the relative positions of the two armies and the movements it was advisable to make. Longstreet gave it as his opinion that the best plan would be to turn Meade's left flank and force him back to the neighborhood of Pipeclay Creek. To this General Lee objected, and pronounced it impracticable under the circumstances.

At the conclusion of the conversation Colonel Long was directed to make a reconnoissance of the Federal position on Cemetery Ridge, to which strong line the retreating troops had retired. This he did, and found that the ridge was occupied in considerable force. On this fact being reported to General Lee, he decided to make no farther advance that evening, but to wait till morning before attempting to follow up his advantage. This decision the worn-out condition of his men and the strength of the position held by the enemy rendered advisable. He turned to Longstreet and Hill, who were present, and said, "Gentlemen, we will attack the enemy in the morning as early as practicable." In the conversation that succeeded he directed them to make the necessary preparations and be ready for prompt action the next day. Longstreet's corps was at that time near Cashtown, but bivouacked for the night on Willoughby's Creek, about four miles from the battlefield.

I will here add that Gettysburg affords a good example of the difficulties to be encountered and the uncertainty of being able to harmonize the various elements of armies when the field of operations is extensive. This battle was precipitated by the absence of information which could only be obtained by an active cavalry force. General Lee had previously considered the possibility of engaging the enemy in the vicinity of Gettysburg, but the time and position were to have been of his own selection. This could have been easily effected had not the cavalry been severed from its proper place with the army.

At a later hour in the evening than that of the events above mentioned the writer had a further conversation with General Lee, which is of sufficient interest to be here narrated. We were then together at the bivouac, under the trees of an apple orchard.

The general, as if he had been thinking over his plans and orders, turned to me with the remark, "Colonel Long, do you think we had better attack without the cavalry? If we do so, we will not, if successful, be able to reap the fruits of victory."

"In my opinion," I replied, "it would be best not to wait for Stuart. It is uncertain where he is or when he will arrive. At present only two or three corps of the enemy's army are up, and it seems best to attack them before they can be greatly strengthened by reinforcements. The cavalry had better be left to take care of itself."

General Lee evidently agreed with me in this opinion. Much as he had been annoyed and his movements hampered by Stuart's absence, the condition of affairs was such that but one judicious course was open. An attack in force on the enemy before he could concentrate his army was very promising of success, and it was with this purpose fully determined upon in the general's mind that the events of that day ended for the Confederate army.

At this stage of the campaign the Count of Paris alludes to the tactics and strategy of

BELOW: Gettysburg and the Baltimore Pike, from Cemetery Hill.

ABOVE: Mrs. Thompson's house, General Lee's headquarters on the Chambersburg Pike.

General Lee in a tone of criticism which calls for some rejoinder on our part. He remarks:

He has four alternatives to select from: He has the choice to retire into the gaps of the South Mountain, in order to compel Meade to come after him; or to wait steadily in his present positions for the attack of the Federals; or, again, to manoeuvre in order to dislodge them from those they occupy by menacing their communications by the right or left; or, finally, to storm these positions in front, in the hope of carrying them by main force. The best plan would undoubtedly have been the first, because, by preserving the strategic offensive, Lee would thus secure all the advantages of the tactical defensive.

Could the count have seen the actual field of operation and have known the circum-stances that governed General Lee, he would probably have taken a different view of his actions.

It must be borne in mind that in entering Pennsylvania without his cavalry General Lee was unable to accumulate supplies. In fact, the subsistence of his army mainly depended on the provisions that could be collected in the vicinity of his line of march by detachments of infantry mounted on artil-lery- and wagon-horses. Therefore, if Lee had adopted the count's preferred plan of operation and occupied one of the passes of South Mountain, he would have placed his army in a trap that would have, in the absence of a miracle, resulted in its destruc-tion; for Meade with his superior forces could have enclosed him without supplies or the means of obtaining them. Lee would thus have been reduced to the alternative of laying down his arms or of cutting his way out with great sacrifice of life and the loss of his artillery and transportation.

The above objection is also applicable to the count's second plan, with the addition that General Lee's line was too much extended to admit of a successful defence against General Meade's superior force. In answer to the count's third plan, it is only necessary to say that the proximity of the two armies and the absence of cavalry on the part of the Confederates rendered manoeuvring impracticable. The fourth is the only one that admitted of the hope of success, and was the one adopted by General Lee.

That the battle may be more clearly described it is necessary to present some of the principal topographical features of the neighborhood of Gettysburg. The town of Gettysburg, nestling in a small valley, is surrounded by numerous low ridges making

various angles with each other. The most important of them is the one situated about a mile south-west, known as Cemetery Ridge. It is terminated by two conical mounds about four miles apart. The one to the south is designated the Round Top. The one to the north is called Culp's Hill.

Immediately after the defeat of the First and Eleventh corps Cemetery Ridge was selected as the Federal position. Nearer the town is a second ridge, nearly parallel to, and about a thousand yards west of, the Cemetery Ridge. This ridge during the battle formed the Confederate centre. From its southern extremity springs obliquely a spur extending almost on a line with the Round Top. This naturally formed the Confederate right. East of the town the valley is traversed by a small stream, beyond which rises abruptly a commanding ridge which was occupied by the Confederate left. The more

ABOVE: Gatehouse to Evergreen Cemetery built at the summit of Cemetery Hill. Union troops fired at attacking Southerners from behind gravestones here.

conflict continued, when the Federal guns began to slacken their fire under the heavy blows of the Confederate batteries, and ere long sank into silence – an example which was quickly followed by the Confederates.

A deathlike stillness then reigned over the field, and each army remained in breathless expectation of something yet to come still more dreadful. In a few moments the attacking column, consisting of Pickett's division, supported on the left by that of Heth commanded by Pettigrew, and on the right by Wilcox's brigade of Anderson's division, appeared from behind a ridge, and, sweeping over its crest, descended into the depression that separated the two armies. The enemy for a moment seemed lost in admiration of this gallant array as it advanced with the steadiness and precision of a review. Their batteries then opened upon it a spasmodic fire, as if recovering from a stunning blow. The force that moved to the attack numbered about 15,000 men. It had a terrible duty to perform. The distance which it was obliged to traverse was more than half a mile in width, and this an open plain in full front of the enemy, who thickly crowded the

crest of the ridge, and within easy range of their artillery.

But the tempest of fire which burst upon the devoted column quickly reduced its strength. The troops of Heth's division, decimated by the storm of deadly hail which tore through their ranks, faltered and fell back in disorder before the withering volleys of the Federal musketry. This compelled Pender's division, which had marched out to support the movement, to fall back, while Wilcox, on perceiving that the attack had failed, fell back, after severe loss, leaving Pickett's men to continue the charge alone. The other supports, Hood's and McLaws's divisions, which had been expected to advance in support of the charging column, did not move, and were too remote to offer any assistance. The consequence was that Pickett was left entirely unsupported.

Yet the gallant Virginians marched steadily forward, through the storm of shot and shell that burst upon their devoted ranks, with a gallantry that has never been surpassed. As they approached the ridge their lines were torn by incessant volleys of musketry as by a deadly hail. Yet with un-

ABOVE: Assault and repulse of George Pickett's Virginians on Cemetery Hill.

OPPOSITE TOP: Scenes of Federal troops in the field, from the opening engagement, at upper left, to withdrawal on July 5, at lower right.

OPPOSITE BOTTOM: The artillery engagement at noon on the third day of battle.

faltering courage the brave fellows broke into the double-quick, and with an irresistible charge burst into the Federal lines and drove everything before them toward the crest of Cemetery Hill, leaping the breastworks and planting their standards on the captured guns with shouts of victory.

The success which General Lee had hoped and expected was gained, but it was a dearly-bought and short-lived one. His plan had gone astray through the failure of the supporting columns. Now was the time that they should have come to the aid of their victorious comrades; but, alas! Heth's division, which had behaved with the greatest gallantry two days before, had not been able to face the terrible fire of the Federal lines, while the other supports were too remote to afford timely relief. The victory which seemed within the grasp of the Confederate army was lost as soon as won. On every side the enemy closed in on Pickett's brigades, concentrating on them the fire of every gun in that part of their lines. It was impossible to long withstand this terrific fusillade. The band of heroes broke and fell back, leaving the greater part of their number dead or wounded upon the field or captive in the hands of their foes.

In justice to Heth's division it must be remembered that on the 1st it was the first to attack the enemy, and maintain an unequal contest until it was reinforced by General Pender with his gallant North Carolinians, and a little later by two divisions of Ewell's corps, and that it continued to oppose the enemy with great gallantry to the close of the action, and suffered heavily both in officers and men, which greatly impaired on the 3d its usual firmness. The brigades of Pender's division had been heavily engaged both on the 1st and 2d, and on the 3d the brigades of Lane and Scales behaved with distinguished gallantry under General Trimble. Wilcox's brigade had gallantly supported Longstreet's attack on the afternoon of the 2nd, and on the 3rd was prevented by difficulties of the ground from keeping pace with the attacking column; and when it was seen that Pickett's attack had failed, it fell back in good order after having sustained heavy loss. All must admit that the troops from the different States were equally distinguished for valor and patriotism.

The Confederates lost in this attack about 4000 men, the most of whom were in Pickett's division. No troops could have behaved better than those of the Army of Northern Virginia on witnessing Pickett's repulse. The officers of every grade on that part of the field exerted themselves with the utmost coolness in preserving order and in endeavoring to re-form the broken ranks, and the men so promptly obeyed the call to rally that their thin ranks were soon restored to order and the whole line was again established. The army was not discouraged or dispirited, and its sole wish was for an opportunity to efface the mortification of its first serious repulse. The desire was general that Meade should assume the offensive and in his turn make an attack, and no doubt was felt of the ability to give him a yet hotter reception than that which Pickett had received. But Meade found his army so much shattered and discouraged by his recent losses that he deemed it inadvisable to attempt to follow up his success.

That this view is correct is proved by the following passage from Mr. William Swinton's *History of the Army of the Potomac*. Mr. Swinton says:

I have become convinced from the testimony of General Longstreet himself that attack would have resulted disastrously. "I had," said that officer to the writer, "Hood and McLaws, who had not been engaged; I had a heavy force of artillery; I should have liked nothing better than to have been attacked, and have no doubt that I should have given those who tried as bad a reception as Pickett received."

OPPOSITE TOP: General Pickett receiving his orders to charge from General Longstreet.

OPPOSITE BOTTOM: At a point in the Union defenses known as the "Angle," General Lewis Armistead, his hat on his sword, destroys a Union battery before being cut down.

BELOW: Amputation at a Federal surgery at Gettysburg. In the fighting, the North suffered some 23,000 casualties and the South about 28,000, taking some 4000 casualties alone during Pickett's attack.

Mr. Swinton further informs us that besides the heavy loss it had sustained by Pickett's attack, the Army of the Potomac was thrown into much confusion by the intermingling of the troops of different divisions and corps. Among the wounded were Major-generals Hancock and Gibbon, two of its most prominent officers. The same writer also informs us that the aggregate loss of the Army of the Potomac during the three days' battle was 23,000 men. Among the officers killed was Major-general J. F. Reynolds, whose gentlemanly bearing and soldierly qualities were unsurpassed in any other officer of either army. In view of this heavy loss, while admitting that General Lee was defeated, it must be acknowledged that Generel Meade was so much crippled that he could not reap any advantage of victory.

The attack of Pickett's division on the 3d has been more criticised, and is still less understood, than any other act of the Gettysburg drama. General Longstreet did not enter into the spirit of it, and consequently did not support it with his wonted vigor. It has been characterized as rash and object-less, on the order of the "charge of the Light Brigade." Nevertheless, it was not ordered without mature consideration and on grounds that presented fair prospects of success. By extending his left wing west of the Emmettsburg road, Meade weakened his position by presenting a weak centre, which being penetrated, his wings would be isolated and paralyzed, so far as regarded supporting each other. A glance at a correct sketch of the Federal position on the 3d will sufficiently corroborate this remark, and had Pickett's division been promptly supported when it burst through Meade's centre, a more positive proof would have been given, for his right wing would have been overwhelmed before the left could have disengaged itself from woods and mountains and come to its relief.

Pickett's charge has been made the subject of so much discussion, and General Lee's intentions in ordering it have been so misunderstood, that it is deemed proper to here offer, in corroboration of what has been said above, the testimony of one who was thoroughly conversant with all the facts.

BELOW: Confederate prisoners, taken at Gettysburg, before being marched to captivity.

Colonel Walter H. Taylor, adjutant-general on the staff of General Lee, in *Southern Historical Society Papers*, vol. iv. p. 83, states as follows:

Later, General Lee rode over to General Ewell's front and conferred as to future movements. He wanted to follow up the success gained – thought that with Johnson's division, then up, that General Ewell could go forward at dawn next day. Ewell, Early, and Rodes thought it best to await Longstreet's arrival and make the main attack on the enemy's left. This was determined on. Longstreet was then about four miles off, with two of his divisions. He was expected early on the morning of the 2d. Orders were sent him to move up to gain the Emmettsburg road. He did not reach the field early, and his dispositions were not completed for attack until four o'clock in the afternoon. In his report General Longstreet says he received orders to move with the portion of his command that was then up, to gain the Emmettsburg road on the enemy's left, but, fearing that he was too weak to attack, he delayed until one of his brigades (Law's) joined its division, and that he began the movement as soon after its arrival as his preparations would admit. It seemed impossible to get the co-operation of the commanders along the line. When Longstreet did attack, he did it in handsome style – drove the enemy and captured prisoners, artillery, and other trophies. So far, we had succeeded in every encounter with the enemy. It was thought that a continuance of the attack as made by Longstreet offered promise of success. He was ordered to renew the fight early on the 3d; Ewell, who was to co-operate, ordered Johnson to attack at an early hour, anticipating that Longstreet would do the same. Longstreet delayed. He found that a force of the enemy occupying high ground on their left would take his troops in reverse as they advanced. Longstreet was then visited by General Lee, and they conferred as to the mode of attack. It was determined to adhere to the plan proposed, and to strengthen him for the movement he was to be reinforced by Heth's division and two brigades of Pender's of Hill's

BELOW: Union soldiers killed in the first days' fighting lie near the Chambersburg Pike.

ABOVE: A young Confederate sniper lies dead in the Devil's Den, a sharpshooters nest at the foot of The Round Top.

corps. With his three divisions which were to attack Longstreet made his dispositions, and General Lee went to the centre to observe movements. The attack was not made as designed: Pickett's division, Heth's division, and two brigades of Pender's division advanced. Hood and McLaws were not moved forward. There were nine divisions in the army; seven were quiet, while two assailed the fortified line of the enemy. A. P. Hill had orders to be prepared to assist Longstreet further if necessary. Anderson, who commanded one of Hill's divisions and was in readiness to respond to Longstreet's call, made his dispositions to advance, but General Longstreet told him it was of no use – the attack had failed. Had Hood and McLaws followed or supported Pickett, and Pettigrew and Anderson been advanced, the design of the commanding general would have been carried out: the world would not

be so at a loss to understand what was designed by throwing forward, unsupported, against the enemy's stronghold so small a portion of our army. Had General Lee known what was to happen, doubtless he would have manoeuvred to force General Meade away from his strong position by threatening his communications with the East, as suggested by –; but he felt strong enough to carry the enemy's lines, and I believe success would have crowned his plan had it been faithfully carried out.

*   *   *

But one course remained open for General Lee. Retreat was necessary. . . . He had still an army of 50,000 men, unbroken in spirit and quite ready to sustain any attack which might be made upon them. But it was quickly evident that Meade had no intention of making an aggressive movement, and a renewed assault on the part of the Confederates would have been madness. . . .

Under these circumstances General Lee determined upon a retreat, but not such an immediate or hasty one as would present the appearance of flight. That he had deeply felt the failure of his effort is unquestionable, yet he preserved much of his ordinary calmness of demeanor, and not one word came from his lips to show that he laid blame on any subordinate . . . .

*   *   *

During the interval between the repulse of Pickett's charge and the night of July 4th . . . General Lee . . . caused the dead to be buried and the severely wounded to be carefully provided for. . . . When it became dark the withdrawal of the army began. First the trains, under protection of Hill's corps, moved out on the Fairfield road; Longstreet followed Hill; then came Ewell, bringing up the rear. The movement was so much impeded by soft roads, darkness, and rains that the rear-guard could not be withdrawn until daylight on the morning of the 5th. General Meade did not attempt to harass the retreating columns of Lee until the rear-guard had reached the neighborhood of Fairfield; then a pursuing column appeared on the neighboring heights, which Early promptly prepared to meet by throwing the rear-guard across its path. After exchanging a few shots the enemy retired, and the retreat was continued . . . .

*   *   *

BELOW: To cover Lee's retreat from Pennsylvannia, railroad tracks were destroyed.

RIGHT: General Meade's August encampment at Culpeper Court-house, Virginia.

The army bivouacked on the night of the 5th in South Mountain Pass, and on the morning of the 6th entered the rich and beautiful Cumberland Valley. . . . Reaching Williamsport on the 7th, and finding his pontoon bridge destroyed and the Potomac swollen far above the fording-point, General Lee occupied a strong position, covering Williamsport and Falling Waters, the point where he had left his bridge on advancing into Pennsylvania. As day after day passed without the appearance of the enemy, General Lee was able to complete his defences, so that when Meade arrived in force on the 12th the Army of Northern Virginia was eager to encounter its old antagonist, though double its numerical strength.

*   *   *

Notwithstanding the Army of the Potomac after its departure from Gettysburg was reinforced to its former numerical strength, General Meade did not attack, but employed the 12th and 13th in fortifying his position. On the other hand, General Lee, now that his bridge was finished and that the river had fallen so as to be fordable for cavalry and empty and lightly-loaded wagons, being unwilling to engage in a battle that could not promise important results, withdrew from his position on the night of the 13th, and retired across the Potomac. The movement was completed during the forenoon of the 14th without interruption, and the broad Potomac rolled between the hostile armies. . . . General Lee continued to retire slowly toward Winchester, and shortly after Meade moved down the river to the neighborhood of Harper's Ferry, and late in July entered Virginia east of the Blue Ridge, whereupon Lee withdrew from the Valley and took a position behind the Rapidan about the 1st of August, while General Meade occupied the neighborhood of Culpeper Court-house.

The losses of the army in killed, wounded, and prisoners were heavy, reaching nearly 16,000 men . . . Having placed the army in position on the Rapidan, and fearing the failure of his campaign in Pennsylvania might have caused the Confederate authorities to lose confidence in him, and feeling unwilling by retaining command of the army to embarrass them in their future plan of operations, General Lee sent his resignation to the President; which was, however, returned by Mr. Davis with every assurance of confidence.

*   *   *

Chapter VII

Wilderness, Spottsylvania, and Cold Harbor

For several weeks both armies remained inactive in the positions they had assumed – Lee on the Rapidan, and Meade in the vicinity of Culpeper Court-house. During that time so many convalescents and other absentees were restored to the ranks that the Army of Northern Virginia, with a small accession from other sources, was raised to a strength of nearly 60,000 men. . . . Within the same period two corps had been detached from the Federal army, . . . This reduction brought the opposing forces more nearly to a numerical equality than had previously been the case, and the change of conditions in his favor induced Lee to make an effort to force Meade to an engagement while his army was reduced in numbers.

*   *   *

In pursuance of his plan of operations, on the 9th of October Lee crossed the Rapidan. . . . Being much retarded by difficult roads, he did not reach his objective point near Culpeper Court-house until the afternoon of the 11th, too late to assail the Federal position that day. Meanwhile, Meade had become aware of the movement of the Confederate army. . . . On the approach of Lee his alert opponent had hastily retired, yet with such

BELOW: Army ambulances leaving for the front. The treatment of wounds had progressed little since the eighteenth century. Nevertheless, many convalescents returned to the ranks.

LEFT: Some of the more than 2000 Confederate soldiers captured by the Federals at Spottsylvania on May 12.

ABOVE: The fight with Stuart's cavalry at Yellow Tavern. Here Jeb Stuart was mortally wounded. Of him, General Lee wrote, "A more zealous, ardent, brave, and devoted soldier than Stuart the Confederacy cannot have."

As Lee retired Gordon put himself at the head of his division and cried out in his ringing voice, "Forward! charge! and remember your promise to General Lee!"

The charge that followed was fierce and telling. . . . The works were retaken, the Confederate line again established, and an impending disaster converted into a brilliant victory.

During the 11th, General Grant was employed in shifting the positions of his corps preparatory to a new assault upon the Confederate lines. Before daylight on the morning of the 12th his army . . . was able to advance unobserved, to break through Johnson's line, and to capture his whole division. . . .

This success inaugurated one of the most desperate conflicts that occurred during the war. The long breach made by the capture of Johnson's division admitted the Federals in heavy masses. . . . From four o'clock in the morning until night the battle continued, marked by terrible slaughter. . . . At last the persistent attacks of the enemy were obliged

to yield to constant repulse and the Federals discontinued the contest.

*   *   *

The succession of bloody combats which had marked the career of Grant in the Wilderness had by this time so greatly reduced his army that he was obliged to pause and await reinforcements.

*   *   *

During the operations about Spottsylvania Court-house, Sheridan conceived the idea of capturing Richmond by a *coup de main*, and on the 9th proceeded to its execution. Of this movement General Stuart quickly became aware, and with his usual promptitude threw himself in Sheridan's path, and encountered him on the 10th at the Yellow Tavern, a few miles north of Richmond. A severe conflict ensued, in which Stuart fell mortally wounded, and his troops were compelled to retire before the superior numbers of the foe.

*   *   *

Sheridan had been so much delayed by Stuart's assault that the small force which had been left for the defence of Richmond had time to reach the works, which were very feebly garrisoned on Sheridan's first approach. He carried the first line, but recoiled from the second, and retired toward the Chickahominy.

* * *

No further effort was made by Grant on the desperately-fought field of Spottsylvania. Having been reinforced by 40,000 reserves, on the 20th of May he disappeared from the front of Lee's army. As in the Wilderness, he began a movement to turn the impregnable position of Spottsylvania by a flank march.

General Lee, however, with his usual alertness, had his men on the march the instant the movement of his adversary was discovered, and he advanced with such rapidity as to reach Hanover Junction, at the intersection of the Fredericksburg and Richmond and the Central railroads, in advance of Grant. This objective point of the Federal army was occupied by Lee on the 22nd. He at once took up a strong position, and when Grant arrived on the 23rd it was to find himself again intercepted by his active opponent.

* * *

General Grant on this occasion did not exhibit his usual pertinacity, but seemed satis-

BELOW: A Timothy O'Sullivan photograph of engineers building a road at Jericho Mill, on the North Anna River, in 1864.

fied by observation alone that the Confederate position could not be carried by main strength. He therefore proceeded down the North Anna to the Pamunkey, which he crossed on the 28th. . . .

*   *   *

Proceeding on his march from the Pamunkey, Grant found his advance upon Richmond again arrested by Lee, . . . Grant did not at this point attempt to force his opponent from his path, but moved slowly by his left flank toward the Chickahominy, while Lee, by a similar movement to his right, kept pace with him and constantly confronted him at every stage.

*   *   *

[By the first of June, the] old battlefield of Cold Harbor was again occupied by the contending forces, though in an inverse order.

The Confederate right now occupied the position that had been previously held by the Federals, and the Federal left held that which had been occupied by the Confederates. This field was about to become the theatre of a second conflict more desperate than the first.

Apparently with the intention of blotting out the memory of the defeat of the Federal arms on the former occasion, General Grant massed the flower of his army for battle. A portion of the Confederate line occupied the edge of a swamp of several hundred yards in length and breadth, enclosed by a low semi-circular ridge covered with brushwood. On the previous night the troops assigned to this part of the line, finding the ground wet and miry, withdrew to the encircling ridge, leaving the breastworks to be held by their picket-line. The attacking column quickly carried this part of the line, and advanced

BELOW: Union cavalry crossing Chesterfield Bridge over the North Anna River, moving toward the battlefield at Cold Harbor.

ABOVE: A. R. Waud's sketch of an artillery duel on June 2 at Cold Harbor.

through the mud and water until arrested by the deliberate fire of the Confederates.

The battle that succeeded was one of the most desperately contested and murderous engagements of the war. Along the whole Federal line a simultaneous assault was made on the Confederate works, and at every point with the same disastrous result. Rank after rank was swept away until the column of assault was almost annihilated. Attack after attack was made, and men fell in myriads before the murderous fire from the Confederate line. While Hill, Breckenridge, Anderson, and Pickett repulsed Grant's desperate assaults upon the right, Early with Rodes, Gordon, and Ramseur on the left successfully opposed Burnside and Warren. In the brief space of one hour the bloody battle of the 3rd of June was over, and 13,000 dead and wounded Federals lay in front of the lines behind which little more than 1000 of the Confederate force had fallen.

A few hours afterward orders were sent to the corps commanders to renew the assault, and transmitted by them through the intermediate channels to the men. Then an event occurred which has seldom been witnessed on a battlefield, yet which testified most emphatically to the silent judgment of the men on the useless slaughter to which they had been subjected. Though the orders to advance were given, not a man stirred. The troops stood silent, but immovable, presenting in this unmistakable protest the verdict of the rank and file against the murderous work decided on by their commanders.

Thus ended Grant's overland campaign, in which his losses aggregated the enormous total of 60,000 men – a greater number than the whole of Lee's army at the beginning of the campaign. Lee's losses, on the contrary, were not more than 20,000. As to the *morale* of the two armies, that of Lee's continued excellent. Their successful defence against their powerful opponent had raised the spirits of the men and their confidence in their general to the highest pitch. On the contrary, the dreadful slaughter to which Grant's army had been subjected produced an inevitable sense of depression in the ranks, and a feeling that they were destined to destruction before the terrible blows of their able antagonist.

It is an error to suppose that in this campaign Lee was afraid to meet his adversary in open field, as had been asserted by Northern writers. He was always ready for action, whether offensive or defensive, under favorable circumstances. "I happen to know," says General Early, "that General Lee had always the greatest anxiety to strike at Grant in the open field." It was the practice of both armies, whenever encamping, to build intrenchments, and it would have been utter folly for Lee to leave his when he found his antagonist willing to attack him behind his breastworks, thus giving him that advantage of a defensive position which the smallness of his army imperatively demanded. Had he advanced against Grant, it would only have been to find the latter behind his works, and the comparative size of the two armies did

not warrant this reversal of the conditions of the contest.

At the beginning of the campaign, perceiving that General Grant's *rôle* was fighting and not manoeuvring, General Lee restrained his desire for the bold and adventurous offensive and strictly confined himself to the defensive, hoping in the course of events to reduce his opponent sufficiently near a physical equality to warrant his attacking him openly with reasonable hope of success. Believing that object had been accomplished after the battle of Cold Harbor, General Lee was anxious to assume the offensive and attack Grant before his army could recover from the stunning effect of its defeat on that occasion; but being obliged to send a large detachment from his army to oppose Sigel and Hunter in the Valley, he was compelled to continue on the defensive.

Grant, on his part, had been taught a costly lesson by his many bloody repulses, and after the battle of Cold Harbor changed his whole plan of operations, deciding to endeavor to accomplish by patient siege what he had failed to achieve by the reckless application of force. With this decision began a new chapter in the history of the war, and one of the most remarkable sieges known to history was inaugurated – that in which the Confederate commander behind the breastworks of Petersburg for a full year baffled every effort of his powerful foe.

* * *

OPPOSITE TOP: Engraving of a cavalry charge at Cold Harbor on June 1.

OPPOSITE BOTTOM: A fruitless assault by New York artillery on the Confederate position on June 3.

BELOW: Collecting remains for reburial long after the battle at Cold Harbor. In the last day's fighting, Grant lost some 13,000 killed and wounded, Lee about 1000.

Chapter VIII

The Siege of Petersburg

The war in Virginia [in 1864] had now been reduced to the attack and defence of Richmond – in other words, to a siege whose termination was only a question of time.

* * *

The battle of Cold Harbor had taught Grant the inutility and peril of direct assaults upon the Confederate intrenchments. He therefore determined upon siege operations, and about the middle of June he threw a large portion of his army south of the James and extended his line of investment so as to embrace the city of Petersburg. This caused Lee to make a counter-movement in order to cover that place and protect the rail-

roads leading to it. The capture of Petersburg was of primary importance to the Federals, as it would enable them to cut of two lines of communication very necessary for the support of Richmond, and at the same time to greatly contract their line of circumvallation. Therefore its possession was much desired.

* * *

General Grant, having failed in his various attempts to force the Confederate lines, acquiesced in a proposal to supplement the musket and the sabre with the spade and the pick. About the last of June it was proposed to mine and blow up a Confederate salient that was opposite to Burnside's position. At

BELOW: From mid-June 1864, the city of Petersburg, a rail center about 25 miles south of Richmond, was the focus of a Federal siege.

that point the two lines were sufficiently near to warrant such an attempt. The conduct of this mining operation was assigned to the person by whom it had been originally proposed, Lieutenant-colonel Henry Pleasants of the Forty-eighth Pennsylvania, a skilful mining engineer. Pleasants found a suitable point to commence operations about five hundred feet distant from the salient to be blown up. His working-parties were drawn from his own regiment, which contained a number of experienced miners. The work was pushed forward so expeditiously that by the 23rd of July the mine was completed, and was charged with 8000 pounds of powder. The tamping was completed and the mine was pronounced ready for explosion by the 28th. It was decided that the mine should be sprung early on the morning of the 30th, and to that end the necessary preparations were made.

General Grant, in order to mask his real design, on the 26th sent Hancock and Sheridan with the Second corps and two divisions of cavalry to the north side of the James River, with instructions to threaten Lee's right, and thus to create the impression that a real attack was to be made in that quarter, while he perfected his arrangements for making the assault on Petersburg upon the explosion of the mine. At this time the Confederate force about Petersburg did not exceed 13,000 men, whilst opposed to this Grant had over 65,000. On the 29th were made the final dispositions for attack.

Hancock was directed on the night of the 29th to return from the north of the James with all secrecy and despatch, and to take part in the assault, while Sheridan was to pass in rear of the army and with his whole cavalry corps operate toward Petersburg from the south and west. On the evening of the 29th, Meade issued his orders of battle. As soon as it was dusk Burnside was to mass

ABOVE: A railroad station near Petersburg. The city defied the Union siege for almost 10 months, until April 3, 1865.

sisting of about 15,000 infantry and 2000 cavalry, into the works along the White Oak road.

Here, on the morning of the 31st, Lee made the flank attack which he had so often attempted with success against the Federal columns. Not waiting for the assault, he boldly took the initiative, and fell upon their exposed flank while they were entangled in the intricacies of a swampy forest. So sudden and heavy was the blow that the divisions encountered hastily gave way. But upon meeting the main body of the Federal troops he found it so thickly massed and well posted as to render an assault hopeless. He therefore fell back to his works.

On the same day Sheridan advanced toward Five Forks. Before reaching that point, however, he was encountered by the Confederate cavalry under the chief command of General Fitz Lee, supported by the infantry under Pickett. A severe combat ensued, in which Sheridan was driven back to Dinwiddie Court-house. . . .

On the 1st of April, Sheridan was reinforced by two corps of infantry, and with this powerful aid he renewed his attack upon Five Forks, which place was carried late in the evening and the Confederates driven back.

General Lee, perceiving that his forces were too weak to combat successfully with the enemy, ordered Longstreet on the afternoon of the 1st to bring his corps with all speed from before Richmond to Petersburg, with the object of supporting his right wing.

Early on the morning of the 2nd the Federals renewed the attack, breaking the lines of the Confederates and forcing them from their position. The Federals then took possession of the Southside Railroad with little opposition, while the Confederates fell back toward Petersburg, followed by the victorious enemy. The pursuit was continued until it was arrested by the guns from two redoubts, Forts Alexander and Gregg, which with great gallantry held the enemy in check until Longstreet came up and interposed his corps, effectually arresting the further advance of the Federal columns.

In the conflict here described fell many gallant warriors, chief among them Lieutenant-general A. P. Hill, who was slain while endeavoring to reach Heth's division, which had been ordered to support Pickett on the right. No man had been more distinguished throughout the war for chivalric bearing than this brave soldier. On every field where appeared the Army of Northern Virginia he had borne a conspicuous part, and now in the last battle of that noble army he found a hero's grave.

BELOW: View of the Appomattox River in April 1865, showing a bridge, railroad cars, and workshops which were burned by the Confederates on evacuating Petersburg.

ABOVE: A Confederate soldier
lies dead at Fort Mahone
after the evacuation of
Petersburg.

LEFT: The occupation of the
Petersburg defenses by
Union troops on April 2, 1865.

357

Chapter IX

Appomattox

The success of the Federal army in breaking the lines of Petersburg had rendered the retreat of the Confederate force imperative. . . . But by abandoning his works and concentrating his army, which still amounted to about 30,000 men, General Lee might retire to some natural stronghold in the interior, where the defensible features of the country would enable him to oppose Grant's formidable host until he could rally strength to strike an effective blow.

*   *   *

Along the north bank of the Appomattox moved the long lines of artillery and dark columns of infantry through the . . . night [of April 2nd], over the roads leading to Amelia Court-house. By midnight the evacuation was completed. . . .

*   *   *

BELOW: Federal columns moving on Richmond. On April 2 whole sections of the Confederate capital were burned by troops preparing to abandon it to the approaching Federals.

The retreat of Lee's army did not long remain unknown to the Federals . . . and they lost no time in taking possession of the abandoned works and entering the defenceless cities. On the morning of the 3rd of April the mayor of Richmond surrendered the city to the Federal commander in its vicinity. . . .

As soon as Grant became aware of Lee's line of retreat he pushed forward his whole available force . . . in order to intercept him on the line of the Richmond and Danville Railroad. . . . Lee pressed on as rapidly as possible to Amelia Court-house, where he had ordered supplies to be deposited for the use of his troops on their arrival. . . . Through an unfortunate error . . . not a single ration was found to be provided for the hungry troops. . . . The only chance remaining to the Army of Northern Virginia was to reach the hill-country without delay. . . . By the morning of the 5th the whole army had

ABOVE: The evacuation of Richmond. Nearly one thousand buildings were destroyed in the fires, and many were damaged.

LEFT: Federal troops entered Richmond on April 3, and raised the Stars and Stripes over the Southern Capitol that morning. Mrs. Robert E. Lee remained in the city under protective guard.

BELOW: General Lee with General Joseph E. Johnston in a photo taken about 1870, the year of Lee's death.

Gen's R. E. LEE and J. E. JOHNSTON.

D. J. Ryan, Savannah, Ga.

harbor until those granite structures crumble into dust.

Perhaps even more important than his work on the Atlantic coast was that on the Mississippi and Des Moines rapids, of which General Meigs, U. S. A., has kindly furnished for this volume a highly interesting account.

The Mexican War opened to him a wider field, and the quick eye of General Scott discovered in the young captain of Engineers "a man of all kinds of merit."

On assuming command in Virginia in April, 1861, General Lee once showed his talents for administration and organization. He found the country almost destitute of the essentials of war, and, as if by magic, he created and equipped an army. His very ability as an organizer made many doubt whether he could be great in other directions, and it was only after successful trial that they were willing to recognize his wonderful versatility.

It was with surprise that they saw him showing himself equal to all the demands made upon him as the commander of a great army in the field. As they looked on, their surprise changed to admiration; the glory of the engineer and organizer was first dimmed, and then eclipsed, by that of the strategist and tactician.

The great soldier is something more than a fighter of battles. He must have a breadth of view sufficient to take in widely-separated movements and to form great and far-reaching combinations. That General Lee had this breadth of view, this subtle intuition, which constitutes the very flower of military genius, is shown by the whole history of the war. The reader will recall how, when he was contemplating an attack on McClellan on the Chickahominy, he sent Jackson to make a vigorous movement in the Valley. He nicely calculated the moral effect of that movement. He intended it to alarm the authorities at Washington – to hold McDowell in position near the Federal capital, and thus prevent his joining in the coming battle.

The Pennsylvania campaign had a wider outlook: it was charged with great possibilities. The defeat of Meade's army in Pennsylvania might be expected to be much more than the simple defeat of that one army. Its effect would be felt on the Mississippi; Grant's army would be needed in the East; the siege of Vicksburg would be raised, and Pemberton's army released for active service. What else might follow it was easy to conjecture. Lee fought, and knew that he

OPPOSITE: General Winfield Scott with his staff. The U.S. Army commander early recognized Lee's military talents.

ABOVE: A Confederate soldier of Company A, 18th Virginia Infantry, in dress uniform.

Ridge for a while seemed successful, then the Muse of History took up her pen to record the birth of a new nation.

Breadth of plan is often neutralized by neglect of details. General Lee did not make that mistake. Before a battle he neglected nothing that might be needful either for attack or defence; in the battle he was quick to see and prompt to meet emergencies. He knew his men, rank and file – what they could do, and how far he might trust them. He was careful to know the ground on which he was to operate, and also to seize and use every advantage of position: he made a league with rivers and mountains and mountain-passes. He studied his adversary, knew his peculiarities, and adapted himself to them. His own methods no one could foresee; he varied them with every change in the commanders opposed to him. He had one method with McClellan, another with Pope, another with Hooker, and yet another with Grant. But for a knowledge of his own resources, of the field, and of his adversary some of his movements might have been rash. As it was, they were wisely bold. Because he was so attentive to details, and guarded so rigidly against the accidents of battle, he was sometimes supposed to be over-cautious; because he sometimes supposed to be over-cautious; because he sometimes attacked greatly superior numbers or divided his forces, he was often thought over-bold. The truth is, that there was in him that harmonious blending of caution and boldness without which a general must often either rashly expose himself to defeat or lose an opportunity for victory.

Whatever other qualities a man may have, he cannot be a great soldier unless he has the power to win the confidence and inspire the enthusiasm of his men. General Lee had this power; few men have had it in a higher degree. No privation or suffering or disaster could shake the confidence of his men in him. In the darkest hour the sight of his form or the mention of his name stirred the hearts of his veterans. They spoke of him with an affection and pride that have not been dimmed by the lapse of years.

It is sometimes said that while General Lee was without a peer in defence, he was not so great in attack. That he was great in defence is witnessed by the series of combats from the Wilderness to Cold Harbor. Hardly anything in the history of warfare, ancient or modern, equals the skill and

fought, for a great stake. That he did not succeed and that the movement came too late, even if it had been successful, to affect the result at Vicksburg, detracts nothing from the brilliancy of the conception. The one pertinent thing is that the Confederate general saw that by a single bold and successful stroke it might be possible virtually to end the war and secure the independence of the Southern Confederacy. That success was possible is shown by the narrow chance by which it failed. It has been well said that when the Confederate charge at Cemetery

Great Seal of the
Confederate States of
America.

LEFT: An engraving of notable
Confederate generals. At
center, Stonewall Jackson;
clockwise from top, Jeb
Stuart, Leonidas Polk, John
B. Magruder, A. P. Hill, James
Longstreet, R. S. Ewell, John
Pemberton, and Sterling
Price.

CHRONOLOGY

January 19, 1807 Robert Edward Lee was born at his family's mansion, Stratford Hall, near Montross, Virginia, the son of Ann Hill Carter and Henry ("Light-Horse Harry") Lee.

January 1, 1808 As required by the U.S. Constitution, the importation of slaves from abroad is ended. But the buying and selling of slaves in the U.S. continues, as does the illegal importation. (The families of both the future wives of Lee and Grant are slave owners.)

1811 Because of his heavy debts, Lee's father moves the family to Alexandria, Virginia. Lee is educated with the intention of enrolling him in West Point.

1812 Lee's father is injured in a Baltimore riot; to aid his recovery he goes (1813) to the Caribbean island of Barbados.

March 25, 1818 On his way home to Virginia, Lee's father dies at the home of his old Revolutionary War comrade, Nathanael Greene, in Cumberland, Georgia.

March 3, 1820 The so-called Missouri Compromise comes into effect with the admission of Missouri as a slave state to balance the admission of Maine as a free state. Also, slavery is forbidden in any of the territory of the Louisiana Purchase above 36° 30'.

April 27, 1822 Hiram Ulysses Grant is born in Point Pleasant, Ohio, to Hannah Simpson and Jesse Root Grant. (When he enters West Point, through an error he is registered as Ulysses Simpson Grant, and he will end up adopting that as his name.)

March 17, 1825 Lee enters West Point.

1828–1835 Grant attends subscription schools in Georgetown, Ohio. He works on the family farm and becomes an expert horseman.

1829 Lee graduates from West Point, 2nd in class of 46 and with no demerits for his four years. He is given the rank of 2nd Lieutenant in the Corps of Engineers and assigned to duty near Savannah, Georgia, where he was to assist in constructing Fort Pulaski. His mother dies within a month after he graduates.

1831 Lee is transferred to Fort Monroe, Virginia, from where he is able to court Mary Anne Randolph Custis. She is the great-granddaughter of Martha Custis Washington by Martha's first marriage, but her father had been adopted by George Washington.

June 30, 1831 Lee marries Mary Custis. They live at her family's home, Arlington, on a hill overlooking Washington, D.C. They will have seven children.

November 1832–March 1833 Certain people in South Carolina have been threatening to nullify the federal tariff acts that they see as favoring northern manufacturing states. They even seem to be threatening to secede on the grounds that states can "nullify" their joining the United States. In December President Andrew Jackson issues a proclamation warning the people of South Carolina that nullification will not be tolerated. In the weeks that follow, Henry Clay and others work to effect a compromise and Jackson signs on to this on March 2nd.

1834–40 Lee serves as Assistant to Chief Engineer of the Army. At first he is assigned to the Office of Engineers in Washington, D.C., but during the following years he sees service on a commission to mark the boundary line between Ohio and Michigan and, on assignment in St. Louis, he participates in a survey and plans for improving navigation of the Mississippi River. He is promoted to 1st Lieutenant in 1836 and to Captain in 1838.

April 1836 North Americans in Texas have revolted against the Mexican government and set up their own republic; their constitution allows for slavery, so these Texans' request to join the United States will be rejected for some years.

June 1839 Grant enters West Point.

1840 Lee returns to the Washington headquarters of the Corps of Engineers.

1841 Lee is placed in charge of improving Fort Hamilton, Fort Lafayette, and other defenses in New York Harbor.

July 1, 1843 Grant graduates from West Point, ranked 21st out of class of 39. He is commissioned a brevet 2nd Lieutenant and assigned to the Fourth Infantry Regiment at the Jefferson Barracks in St. Louis, Missouri.

February 1844 Grant meets Julia Dent, sister of his West Point roommate, Frederick Dent.

May 1844 Grant's regiment is ordered to the Louisiana border of Texas. After a leave during which he proposes marriage to Julia Dent, he joins his regiment there in June.

June 1844 Lee is briefly assigned to West Point on its Board of Visitors.

March 1845 The U.S. Congress has passed a joint resolution accepting Texas as a state.

May 1845 Recently inaugurated President James Polk, determined to make Texas a state, orders Gen. Zachary Taylor with a detachment of the U.S. Army to guard the border of southeastern Texas against an "invasion" by Mexico.

September 1845 Grant's unit moves on to Corpus Christi, Texas, where it becomes part of the army being assembled by Gen. Taylor.

December 1845 Texas is admitted as a state. Grant is promoted to full 2nd Lieutenant.

March–May 1846 Under orders from President Polk, Gen. Taylor leads his troops over to the left bank of the Rio Grande, always recognized as Mexican Territory. Grant's regiment goes with this force. Taylor proceeds to build fortifications near Matamoros. When Mexican forces attack this so-called Fort Texas, Taylor's forces engage the Mexicans in two battles—Palo Alto (May 8) and Reseca de la Palma (May 9). Grant first experiences combat at Palo Alto and briefly leads his company in Battle of Resaca de la Palma.

May 13, 1846 President Polk signs the War Bill (passed by Congress on May 11–12) declaring that "a state of war exists" with Mexico.

August 19–September 24, 1846 With his 4th Infantry Regiment, Grant sets off with Gen. Taylor on his pursuit of the Mexican army to Monterrey, which the US forces capture on September 24.

August 1846–January 1847 Lee joins the staff of Gen. John E. Wool in San Antonio, Texas. He accompanies Wool's force as it moves toward Chihuahua in northern Mexico. Lee's duties are those of an engineer—bridge-building and road repair—but he also engages in some reconnoitering.

December 1846 Grant's unit is assigned to the mouth of the Rio Grande, where Gen. Winfield Scott is assembling an invasion force that will eventually march on Mexico City.

February 1847 Lee is transferred to Brazos, Mexico, where he joins the staff of Gen. Winfield Scott, now preparing for the landing at Vera Cruz and the march to Mexico City.

March 9–28, 1847 Scott's forces make an amphibious invasion of the coast surrounding Vera Cruz. Lee is responsible for setting up the artillery batteries that lead to the city's surrender. Grant also participates in the siege that ends with the city's surrender on March 28th.

April 8, 1847 Scott sends his first units out on the 260-mile march to Mexico City. Both Grant and Lee are part of this force. Grant is now the quartermaster of his regiment. but will always try to get into the thick of the action during engagements with the enemy. Lee distinguishes himself by his bold reconnaissance.

April 17–18, 1847 The first US units have moved about 50 miles inland to Cerro Gordo ("big hill"), where they meet heavy resistance from the Mexicans. Lee makes the reconnaissances and in three days' time places batteries in positions that Gen. Santa Anna had judged inaccessible, enabling Scott to carry the heights and rout the enemy. Grant also participates in this battle.

May 15, 1847 After subduing relatively light resistance from the Mexican forces, the American army takes Puebla, a large city on the road to Mexico City. Grant participates in this action; Lee enters the city two weeks later with Gen. Scott and his staff.

August 7, 1847 US forces depart Puebla for Mexico City. Grant is part of the advance force. Lee will follow several days later with staff of Gen. Scott. All along the way to Mexico City, Lee will perform valuable advance reconnaissances.

August 17–19, 1847 US forces take the well-fortified villages of San Augustin and San Antonio. Lee has scouted ahead for the best routes and then participates in the action. Grant also takes part in this action.

August 20, 1847 US forces engage in fierce battles at Contreras and Churubusco. Both Grant and Lee participate. Gen. Scott will later single out Lee for "the greatest feat of physical and moral courage performed by any individual in my knowledge." Lee himself, reporting on the brave actions of the various officers in these battles, referred to "Lieutenant Grant, regimental quartermaster, who was usefully employed in his appropriate duties."

September 8, 1847 Both Grant and Lee participate in the battle at Molino del Rey. Lee is promoted to brevet Lieutenant-Colonel.

September 12–13, 1847 Grant and Lee participate in the Battle for Chapultepec, the last major fortress guarding Mexico City. In the storming of Chapultepec, Lee is slightly wounded, and due to total exhaustion, faints; after Chapultepec Lee was recommended for the rank of colonel. During the battle, as the American forces approached the gate of San Cosme at the outskirts of Mexico City, they were stopped by Mexican artillery. Grant leads his unit around to one side and has a howitzer carried up into a church belfry, from which point he is able to fire down on the Mexicans. He will be cited by Gen. Scott for this action. That night the first American troops begin to enter Mexico City

September 14, 1847 Gen. Scott leads the American forces into the main plaza of Mexico City for a surrender ceremony. Lee is at his side. Grant is among the troops who move through the city.

September 16, 1847 Grant is promoted to 1st Lieutenant. He will be stationed on the edge of Mexico City as part of the occupation forces. Lee is stationed in Mexico City at the headquarters of the occupation forces.

February 1848 The United States signs the Treaty of Guadalupe Hidalgo with Mexico, ending the war and taking over vast territory that will eventually become the states of California, Nevada, Utah, most of New Mexico and Arizona, and parts of Colorado and Wyoming. Texas is also conceded to belong to the United States. This new land will lead to disputes between pro- and anti-slavery forces.

June 1848 Lee returns to the United States and is assigned to the headquarters of the Corps of Engineers in Washington.

July 23, 1848 Grant arrives back in the United States and goes on extended leave.

August 22, 1848 Grant marries Julia Dent of St. Louis, Missouri. They will have four children.

November 17, 1848–52 Following his honeymoon, Grant reports to duty at Detroit, Michigan, and from there is assigned to Sackets Harbor, New York, on the eastern shore of Lake Ontario. In April 1849 he returns to regimental headquarters in Detroit. Grant is reassigned to Sackets Harbor in June 1851.

During this same time, Lee is assigned to the Corps of Engineers at Fort Carroll in Baltimore Harbor and is charged with constructing defense works to supplement those at Fort McHenry.

September 9–12, 1850 After months of negotiation, Congress adopts—and President Millard Fillmore signs—the five bills that come to be known as the Missouri Compromise. They allow for the admission of California as a no-slavery state but recognize the rights of other territories to allow slavery. Although the slave trade in the District of Columbia will be abolished, another act strengthens the federal enforcement of the Fugitive Slave Act.

June 1851 *Uncle Tom's Cabin*, by Harriet Beecher Stowe, begins to appear as a serial novel in the *National Era*, an anti-slavery paper.

1852–54 In May 1852, Grant is assigned to San Francisco. Arriving there in August, he is assigned to remote posts, first at Fort Vancouver on the Columbia River, and then (1853) to Humboldt Bay, California. The combination of the isolation, separation from his family, and a dislike for his commanding officer leads Grant to decide to resign from the army. He submits his resignation on April 11, 1854, the same day he is notified of promotion to Captain.

1852–55 Lee—at first reluctantly—serves as the ninth Superintendent of West Point Academy. Although he never totally enjoys the position, his tenure proves to be successful and respected.

1854–58 In August 1854, Grant returns to Missouri and joins Julia and his children. He moves to a 60-acre farm near St. Louis that belongs to Julia but depends on selling cut firewood for supporting his family.

1855–61 Lee is appointed Lieutenant Colonel of the Second Cavalry and serves in Texas in wars against the Kiowa and Comanche Indians there. At various times he returns home to Virginia to take care of family matters.

1858–59 Having failed at farming, Grant works at selling real estate with a cousin of Julia's, but this, too, proves unsuccessful.

October 17–18, 1859 On one of his visits home from Texas, Lee is assigned to lead a U.S. Marine detachment to Harpers Ferry, Virginia, where he puts down the insurrection led by John Brown.

May 1860 Grant moves to Galena, Illinois, to work as a clerk in his father's leather store.

1860–61 Lee is assigned to command of the Department of Texas.

November 6, 1860 Abraham Lincoln is elected president.

December 20, 1860 South Carolina is the first state to secede from the Union. In the ensuing weeks, ten more states will also secede and form the Confederacy.

January 23, 1861 Following the events unfolding in the South from Texas, Lee writes his son Custis, "The South, in my opinion, has been aggrieved by the acts of the North." But at this same time he writes to another son, Rooney: "As an American citizen I prize the Union very highly and know of no personal sacrifice that I would not make to preserve it, save that of honour."

March 16, 1861 Texas having seceded from the Union (Feb. 1), Lee has returned to Arlington, Virginia. He is appointed colonel of First Cavalry.

April 12–13, 1861 After 32 hours of bombardment from Confederate batteries, Fort Sumter in the harbor of Charleston, South Carolina, surrenders.

April 18, 1861 Through Lincoln's emissaries, Lee is offered the command of United States Armies. Lee refuses the offer by stating: "I cannot raise my hand against my birthplace, my home, my children…."

April 20, 1861 Lee resigns commission in United States Army.

April 23. 1861 Lee accepts rank of Brigadier General and is placed in command of all of Virginia's military and naval forces as Virginia secedes and joins the Confederacy.

April 29, 1861 Grant becomes military aide to Illinois governor Richard Yates

May–July, 1861 Lee organizes troops and advises President Jefferson Davis in Richmond.

June 15–28, 1861 Grant is appointed commander of the militia infantry regiment; on the 17th he is appointed its colonel; on the 28th, the regiment is taken into the U.S. Army's service as the 21st Illinois Volunteers.

July 1861 After training his regiment, Grant leads them into Missouri to perform guard duties.

August 5, 1861 Grant is appointed Brigadier General.

August–October, 1861. Lee is in charge of abortive campaign in the western counties of Virginia. His lack of success there—most especially at Cheat Mountain—temporarily damages his reputation as a field commander.

September 1, 1861 Grant is appointed commander of the District of Southeast Missouri and establishes his headquarters at Cairo, Illinois.

November 1861 Lee is placed in charge of coast defenses in South Carolina, Georgia, and Florida.

November 7, 1861 In his first combat engagement as a general, Grant leads a raid on the Confederate camp at Belmont, Missouri; his troops stop to loot the camp and the Confederates regroup, so Grant has to withdraw.

February 6–16, 1862 In the first Union victory of strategic importance, Grant takes Fort Henry and Fort Donelson, both in Tennessee. His message to the besieged Confederate forces in Fort Donelson—"No terms except immediate and unconditional surrender can be accepted"—soon makes him nationally famous as "Unconditional Surrender" Grant.

March 1862 Lee is recalled to Richmond by Jefferson Davis and becomes the president's military advisor. Lee will soon find himself organizing the defenses of Richmond, and as Gen. George McClellan's Federal forces start their campaign on the Peninsula, Lee plans the diversionary campaign of Gen. Thomas "Stonewall" Jackson in the Shenandoah Valley.

April 6–7, 1862 Grant meets the Confederate forces at the Battle of Shiloh (so named after a church in the battlefield). In two days of extremely bloody fighting, the Union troops suffer higher casualties but force the Confederates to start retreating from Tennessee.

June 1, 1862 In McClellan's Peninsular Campaign, Confederate General J.E. Johnston is severely wounded at the battle of Seven Pines (Fair Oaks). Lee assumes command of the Army of Northern Virginia.

June 25–July 2, 1862 Lee commands the Confederate forces in the Seven Days' Battles that force McClellan away from Richmond and back down the Peninsula. But Lee is unable to destroy the Union forces.

July–November 1862 Grant has been given command of all Union troops between the Mississippi and Tennessee and moves his headquarters to Corinth, Mississippi. For the next four months, he will be occupied largely in command duties. Not until November 2 does Grant move out into the field again in what is the beginning of a long campaign to capture Vicksburg, Mississippi.

August 30, 1862 Lee defeats Union forces under Gen. John Pope at Second Manassas (Second Bull Run).

September 5–16, 1862 Lee crosses the Potomac and begins to advance into Maryland. He and his forces fight a series of battles along the way.

September 17, 1862 Along Antietam Creek, near Sharpsburg, Maryland, Lee's forces confront the Federals commanded by Gen. McClellan. At the end of what is known as "the bloodiest single day of the war" (and probably in American history), the battle ends in a draw. On the 18th, however, Lee is persuaded to withdraw, and in so doing the Confederate cause takes a major turn for the worse.

December 13. 1862 At Fredericksburg, Virginia, Lee commands a masterful defeat of the Federal forces under Gen. Ambrose Burnside.

December 1862 Lee moves his forces into winter quarters until March.

February–April 1863 Grant commands a series of unsuccessful attempts to take Vicksburg, Mississippi.

May 2–3, 1863 At Chancellorsville, Virginia, Lee again commands a decisive victory over the Union forces under Gen. Joseph Hooker, but Lee's strongest general, "Stonewall" Jackson, is wounded and dies on May 10th.

May 12–22, 1863 As part of his strategy to take Vicksburg, Grant moves his forces between two Confederate armies and ends up defeating them both in battles at Jackson, Champion Hill, and Big Black River. His final assaults on the city (May 19th–22nd) fail, and he settles down for a long siege.

June 3–30, 1863 Lee initiates his plan to invade the North and moves north from Fredericksburg, Virginia, into southern Pennsylvania.

July 1–3, 1863 At Gettysburg, in three days of aggressive fighting, although the Confederates are conceded to have won the first two days' battles, they are defeated on the third day and brought to a halt with "Pickett's Charge."

July 4, 1863 Grant accepts the Confederate forces' surrender of Vicksburg. The Confederacy is now virtually cut in half at the Mississippi, and large Federal forces under Grant and others are freed for other campaigns.

July 4–13, 1863 The inaction of the Federals at Gettysburg, commanded by Gen George Meade, allows Lee to retreat and get back across the Potomac with all his forces.

August 1863 Following a fall from a horse in New Orleans, Grant spends the summer with his family in a house near Vicksburg. His leg is so badly swollen that he is bedridden for weeks and uses crutches until October.

August 8, 1863 Because of the criticism following the defeat at Gettysburg, Lee hands in his resignation to President Davis, who refuses to accept it.

October 23–November 25, 1863 After the defeat of the Union forces at Chickamauga, Union Gen. William Rosecrans retreats to Chattanooga, Tennessee, where he is soon besieged. Grant is now ordered to relieve the siege and arrives outside Chattanooga on October 23rd. After a series of major battles, culminating in the one at Missionary Ridge, Grant drives the Confederates from the field.

October 9–November 9, 1863 Lee conducts the Bristoe Campaign; during several engagements, Lee forces the vastly superior Union forces of Gen. Meade to retreat.

November 26–December 1, 1863 Gen. Meade launches an offensive against Lee, but fails to dislodge the Confederates along the Mine Run. Following this, both armies go into winter quarters.

March 3–12, 1864 Grant is ordered to report to Washington D.C. (on the 3rd) where he has been confirmed as a Lieutenant General, the highest rank at that time. On the 9th, he is given his commission by President Lincoln himself and on March 12, he is appointed General-in-Chief of all U.S. armies.

May 5–7, 1864 Grant has taken to the field to direct the Federal Army of the Potomac in what is hoped will be a quick campaign to take Richmond, the Confederate capital. During the Battle of the Wilderness, Grant and Lee face each other for the first time as commanders. The battle itself is something of a draw, but although the Union forces lose twice as many men as the Confederates, the North can better afford to make up its losses.

May 7–20, 1864 In the Spotsylvania campaign, Grant is once again thwarted by Lee, and the results of the battle are inconclusive. On May 11, Grant writes another of his famous dispatches: "I propose to fight it out on this line if it takes all summer."

May 21–June 1, 1864 Lee conducts operations on interior lines.

May 31–June 3, 1864 The Battle of Cold Harbor. In the main frontal assault on June 3, Grant loses 7000 men in an hour. Lee loses 1500. Grant will admit that this was one of his greatest blunders as a general. Again, although the Federal casualties greatly exceed those of the Confederate—50,000 vs 32,000— the North can more readily provide replacements.

June 15–July 30, 1864 Grant has decided to try a new approach to taking Richmond: he wants to capture Petersburg, the major rail junction south of Richmond and so cut it off. In order to exercise close command, he relocates his headquarters to City Point, Virginia, along the James River, 10 miles from Petersburg. The first direct assaults fail (June 15th–18th). Lee himself arrives in Petersburg on the 18th. The Union forces decide to resort to a siege instead of assaults, but they do attempt the ill-fated explosion of the subterranean mine they have dug; the explosion occurs on July 30 and creates a giant crater, but the Union forces who then attempt to advance are repulsed at great cost of lives. Although Lee was not on the scene that day, he did approve the operation. Lee himself directs this defense.

August 1864–April 1865 In the months following the disastrous mine assault, a whole series of battles are fought around Petersburg and Richmond.

February 9, 1865 Newly appointed commander-in-chief of all Confederate forces, Lee issues his first general order.

April 2–3, 1865 In the final Union assault on Petersburg, the Confederates have to abandon the city during the night of April 2–3. Grant enters the city on the 3rd. During the day of the 2nd, Lee also has to leave Richmond and it is occupied by Union forces on the 3rd.

April 3–9, 1865 Lee heads southwest, hoping to elude the Federals and join up with the Confederate forces operating in North Carolina. Grant leads the pursuit and soon has Lee's army in disarray and then trapped. On the 7th, Grant writes to Lee and asks that he surrender his forces.

April 9, 1865 At Appomattox Court House in Virginia, in the home of Wilmer McClean, Lee surrenders his Army of Northern Virginia to Grant. Although hostilities continue elsewhere for some time, this effectively marks the end of the Civil War.

April 10, 1865 Lee issues his Farewell Address to the Army of Northern Virginia.

May 1865–May 1868 Grant retains his post as head of the U.S. Army (Congress promotes him to full General in 1866), but he carries on a series of visits to various cities throughout the nation that amount to a virtual triumphal tour—and clearly mark him as presidential material. At first he supports President Andrew Johnson's policies with the former Confederate states, but gradually he begins to separate himself from Johnson.

June 13, 1865 Lee applies for pardon. His home in Arlington, Virginia, is confiscated by the Union Army (and is now part of Arlington National Cemetery). Although there is some call in the North for trying Lee as a traitor, it never comes to pass, but his civil rights are suspended and his United States citizenship is withdrawn. (Grant signed the oath of allegiance to the United States that was required before a pardon could be granted, but it was misplaced and did not surface until 1970. Lee's full citizenship was restored by Congress and President Gerald Ford in 1975.)

August 4, 1865 Lee is elected President of Washington College, Lexington, Virginia. (After his death it will be renamed Washington and Lee University.)

February 4, 1867 Lee declines to be a candidate for the governorship of Virginia.

May 21, 1868 Grant is nominated as a candidate for president by the Republican National Convention in Chicago. During the summer, Grant hardly strays from his home in Galena, Illinois, and does little active campaigning.

November 3, 1868 Grant is elected president by a landslide.

March 4, 1869 Grant is inaugurated President of the United States. During his first four years in office, although he does work for reconciliation between the North and South and to protect the rights of the newly freed African Americans, Grant seems powerless as corruption spreads through all levels of the government. Part of it is due to the "spoils system," under which the party in power gets to appoint its supporters, friends, and relatives to government jobs. Grant himself does not profit from any of this, but when it is revealed that his brother-in-law has promised financial speculators that he can get Grant to hold off selling gold, Grant is tainted even thought the plot fails.

March–April, 1870 In failing health, Lee visits Georgia in search of convalesence.

October 12, 1870 Lee dies at his home in Lexington, Virginia. He is buried in the chapel on the campus of Washington and Lee University.

November 5, 1872 Grant is elected by an even larger majority. Again, his term is marred by a financial panic (1873) and a series of financial scandals. Grant again remains largely untouched by the corruption, although he is revealed to have accepted some personal gifts. He remains so popular, though, that the Republicans urge him to run for a third term, but he declines.

May 1877–September 1879 Grant takes his family on a trip around the world. Everywhere he goes, he is greeted by crowds.

June 2–8, 1880 Grant is unsuccessful in securing the Republican nomination for President. It is generally conceded that he was really not desirous of holding office again.

December 24, 1883 Grant suffers a serious injury to his hip; he will walk with crutches or a cane for the rest of his life.

May 1884 The brokerage firm of Grant and Ward fails on Wall Street, and Grant will lose his entire fortune. He had been a silent partner in the firm with his son and Ferdinand Ward, who robbed the company and was eventually jailed. Days before the bankruptcy, Ward begs Grant for a loan of $150,000 to save the Marine Bank. Grant raises the money through a personal loan from multimillionaire William Vanderbilt; he eventually repaid Vanderbilt with his war trophies and uniforms (some of which are on display in the Smithsonian). The Grant and Ward failure plunges Grant into a prolonged depression.

September 1884 Grant is diagnosed as having cancer of the throat. Realizing that he will not have long to live, and wanting to leave his wife some money to live on, he soon begins work on his memoirs.

January–March, 1885 The cancer has spread and Grant is now in great pain, barely able to eat liquid food. He continues to write.

June 16, 1885 Grant moves with his family to Mt. McGregor, near Saratoga Springs, New York, because of the cooler climate. He is down to 120 pounds weight and is extremely weak.

July 10, 1885 Grant finishes his memoirs. All this time he has also been reading page proofs of as fast as the printers have been sending them to him.

July 23, 1885 At 8:00 AM, Grant dies, surrounded by his family and physicians. Eventually (1897) his body will be interred in the monumental tomb above the Hudson River on upper Manhattan Island, New York City. The tomb was paid for by private subscriptions.

Autumn 1885 The first of the two volumes of *Personal Memoirs of U.S. Grant* is published. It quickly becomes a best seller, and in Julia's remaining lifetime over 300,000 copies are sold, earning his widow an estimated $450,000 (the equivalent of at least 10 times that in terms of buying power today).

Memoirs of Robert E. Lee, by Armistead Long, is published. Although it is well received, it never attains the status of Grant's memoirs.